Better Homes and Gardens®

celebrate the SEASON®

2003

Better Homes and Gardens® Books
Des Moines, Iowa

Better Homes and Gardens® Creative Collection™

Celebrate the Season®2003

Director, Editorial Administration
Michael L. Maine

Editor-in-Chief
Beverly Rivers

Editorial Manager   **Art Director**
Ann Blevins   Brenda Drake Lesch

Managing Editor
Karman Wittry Hotchkiss

Associate Art Director	Kimberly Morgan
Associate Art Director	Shawn Roorda
Food Editor	Julia Martinusen
Copy Chief	Mary Heaton
Administrative Assistant	Lori Eggers
Contributing Editor	Jilann Severson
Contributing Projects Editor	Heidi Palkovic
Contributing Photo Stylists	Jill Budden, Marisa Dirks
Contributing Writers	Sharyl Heiken, Carol McGarvey
Contributing Copy Editors	Gretchen Kauffman, Ann Klein
Contributing Proofreaders	Susan J. Kling, Katherine Nugent, Joleen Ross
Contributing Indexer	Stephanie Reymann
Test Kitchen Director	Lynn Blanchard
Test Kitchen Product Supervisor	Jill Moberly

Vice President, Publishing Director
William R. Reed

Group Publisher	Maureen Ruth
Cons. Prod. Sr. Marketing Manager	Steve Swanson
Business Director	Christy Light
Business Manager	Jie Lin
Production Director	Douglas M. Johnston
Books Production Managers	Pam Kvitne, Marjorie J. Schenkelberg, Rick von Holdt
Assistant to the Publisher	Cheryl Eckert

MEREDITH PUBLISHING GROUP

Publishing Group President	Stephen M. Lacy
Magazine Group President	Jerry Kaplan
Corporate Solutions	Michael Brownstein
Creative Services	Ellen de Lathouder
Manufacturing	Bruce Heston
Consumer Marketing	Karla Jeffries
Finance and Administration	Max Runciman

Meredith
CORPORATION

Chairman and CEO   William T. Kerr

In Memoriam   E.T. Meredith III (1933–2003)

Our seal assures you that every recipe in *Celebrate the Season* has been tested in the Better Homes and Gardens® Test Kitchen. This means that each recipe is practical and reliable and meets our high standards of taste appeal. We guarantee your satisfaction with this book for as long as you own it.

For editorial questions, please write:

BETTER HOMES AND GARDENS®
Celebrate the Season, 1716 Locust Street, Des Moines, IA 50309-3023.

Crafts.
Discover life's little pleasures.

take comfort in tradition. Familiar

rituals, decorations, and foods bring us back to memories of happy holidays

spent with family and friends. Each year as we unpack the decorations and

pull out the recipe cards, our thoughts return to times we always seem to

recall as simpler. Whether those days were indeed more slowly paced is hard

to tell. At *Better Homes and Gardens® Creative Collection™*, what we do

know is how to create stylish and updated decorations, gifts, and foods that

honor our favorite seasons without taking every second of our spare time.

On these pages, we offer adornments and gifts that make the best use of

new crafting materials and foods that take advantage of shortcut techniques.

We'll help you find time to renew old friendships, retell treasured stories, and

even relax a little. This holiday season, let the ideas on the following pages

help you and your family find **a quiet calmness.**

Beverly Rivers

— Beverly Rivers, Editor

table of contents

setting the stage

gathering together

giving from the heart

kids' stuff

4

In a Twinkling

Easy-to-use ideas for the holidays

SETTING THE STAGE

Blend old and new in your holiday decorating this year. Give a fresh look to wreaths and greenery by adding unusual materials to the standard pine and fir boughs, make stockings from unexpected materials, and update acorns and pumpkins with pearls and paint. On the following pages, you'll find trees of every size and color so no room will go unadorned. Check out the ornaments you can make in a flash, and don't miss the candles and other accessories that beg for festive dress-ups.

forever greens

There's nothing like the smell of fresh greenery to trigger dreams of the holidays. Many wreaths, garlands, and other embellishments hold their welcoming appeal long after the Christmas season passes, extending the warmth of the holidays well into the New Year.

Wreaths and garlands add a festive touch to your home but they do have their hang-ups, especially when you do not want to damage your wall or stair rail. Removable self-adhesive hooks can be used to hang many wreaths and will eliminate having to pound nails in the wall. Wreath hangers work well on most doors. Attach garlands to handrails with chenille strips or ribbon rather than wire to avoid damaging the rail's finish.

selecting greens

Almost any type of fresh greenery can be used to make wreaths or garlands. The texture and stiffness of the needles and stems will determine the final shape of your project. Softer greens, such as cedar, create a graceful garland that drapes easily or a wreath that has a feathery appearance. Stiffer greens, such as fir or short-needled pine, have lots of body and will give a more solid appearance to both garlands and wreaths. Leafy greens, such as salal or boxwood, should be scaled to the size of the project. Because its leaves are diminutive, boxwood works best for smaller projects or when the surface is tightly curved. Salal leaves cover a large area quickly so work best for bigger projects. Both boxwood and salal are available through florists.

Check tree lots for bundles of greens ready for use in wreaths or garlands. For large projects, florists or mail-order tree companies often sell boxes of mixed greens. Trimmings from your own tree or the trees and shrubs in your yard often work for small projects. Never trim branches from public places. For simple projects like the wreath shown *opposite*, don't overlook premade wreaths. They often save both time and money.

vintner's dream wreath

Concentric rings of pine, cedar, and champagne grapes give a bit of a twist to wreaths packed with greens and cranberries. The elegant look is perfect for a dining room or formal entry. High-quality artificial grapes look real and will last the whole season without wilting or bleeding.

Wire bunches of artificial champagne grapes to the innermost ring of a 14-inch four-wire box wreath. Pack the grapes tightly until they form a solid band 2 to 3 inches wide.

Clip pine or spruce boughs into small branches. If necessary, wire the stems to the wreath form. Insert the stems between the outer wires of the wreath form. See the photograph *opposite* for details. Clip small branches of cedar, and insert them over the pine and under the grapes.

tutti-frutti wreath

A beautiful wreath packed with dried oranges, lemons, limes, kumquats, and artichokes presents a nature-inspired welcome, especially when embedded in fresh bay leaves. The citrus scent will fill the air for a week or two after displaying. By freeze-drying some of the elements, the wreath will last longer, but to ensure the longest life, keep it away from heat as much as possible. The best results will come from displaying it outdoors in the cool winter air. Artificial fruits can be substituted as desired.

Make a small hole in the bases of the freeze-dried oranges, limes, and lemons (you will need five of each). Cut 6-inch lengths of small twigs and hot-glue the twigs into the holes. Allow all the elements to cool.

Cut short lengths of bay leaves and wrap several stems together with fine-gauge paddle-style florist's wire. Attach the loose end of the wire to a rung of the 18-inch wire wreath form. Add another bundle of leaves over the stems of the first bundle and wire it in place. Repeat this process until the entire wreath form is covered. Work so that the leaves all face one direction and no stems or wires are visible.

To attach the fruit, twist a length of wire around the twig ends of each orange, lemon, and lime. Twist the wire to the wreath, spacing each fruit evenly around the display. Wrap a length of wire around the bases of five or six dried mini artichokes, then attach them to the wreath. Hot-glue 15 to 18 freeze-dried kumquats evenly around the wreath.

Trim all the wires and turn the ends into the wreath to prevent scratching the door or wall. Rotate the wreath daily as the bay leaves dry so that one side doesn't flatten.

10

tutti-frutti garland

Glossy lemon or salal leaves offer a charming alternative to traditional evergreen garland and are especially appropriate as the foundation for a Williamsburg-style citrus arrangement. The fruits should last a week or two in a cool environment; then they will need to be replaced or discarded.

Clip small branches of lemon or salal leaves so each branch is about 6 inches long and has five to seven leaves. Cut ½-inch-diameter sisal rope to the desired length for the garland. Twist the end of florist's paddle wire to one end of the rope. Gather several branches and wire the stems to the rope.

Lay another cluster of branches over the wire to cover the stems of the first bundle and secure it in place with the wire. Repeat until all the rope is covered with leaves. For the last bundle, turn it backwards so that the stems are away from the rope end. Slide the stems under the previous leaves and wire the bundle in place.

Slide 12-inch lengths of heavy florist's wire through small oranges, lemons, limes, and kumquats. Twist the wire to the back of the fruit and attach the fruit to the garland. Cluster most of the fruits at the end, and then taper them off down the length of the garland. See the photograph *above* for details.

For the cinnamon sticks, cut wire twice the length of each cinnamon stick plus 8 inches. Slide the wire up through the hollow of one side of a cinnamon stick and back down through the hollow of the other side, forming a hairpin shape that goes through the cinnamon stick. Repeat this for each cinnamon stick. Group three cinnamon sticks and twist the wires together. Wire the cinnamon stick clusters to the garland. Trim the wire ends and tuck them into the garland to prevent scratching the wood.

souper idea

Use a soup tureen or another pretty container to create a topiary fit for a sideboard, buffet, or tabletop. A cone of florist's foam provides the structure for the boxwood, berries, and fruits.

Cut a few inches from the top of a floral foam cone, creating a platform for the pineapple. Secure the cone in the bottom of the container with florist's wax. Pierce the bottom of a small pineapple with two or more bamboo skewers, placing them close to the core of the pineapple. Leave several inches extending beyond the bottom of the pineapple. Slide the skewers into the top of the cone to hold the pineapple in place. Further secure the pineapple with florist's wire and tape or hot glue.

Insert shortened skewers or florist's picks into lemons, limes, oranges, or other fruits. Insert the picks into the cone. Add dabs of hot glue to further secure the fruit. Fill in the remaining spaces with sprigs of boxwood, berries, and salal or lemon leaves. Tuck additional greens into the tureen to cover any open spots.

11

boxwood ball with twig tassel

Give a new twist to the traditional kissing ball. Cover it with boxwood instead of mistletoe, then add a twig tassel. Ours is small, but make yours any size you want by using any size of plastic-foam ball. If you alter the size, keep the proportions right by cutting the twigs about three times the diameter of the ball.

here's how

Cut a 14-inch length of medium-gauge wire to serve as a hanger. Fold it in half (hairpin style), dip the ends in tacky crafts glue, and insert the ends into a 6-inch-diameter plastic-foam ball.

Coat sections of the ball with tacky crafts glue, then cover the ball with moss. See the photograph *below* for details. Repeat until the entire ball is covered. U-shaped florist's pins also can be used to attach the moss.

Cut 8 to 10 twigs about 18 inches long each. Dip the ends into tacky crafts glue and insert them opposite the hanger.

Cut fresh boxwood into 3- to 4-inch lengths. Insert the boxwood into the ball, packing it tightly so the ball is entirely covered. If desired, dip the end of each stem into glue before inserting it into the ball. Tie a ribbon at the top.

with bells on

Moss-covered bells ring in the holidays silently and peacefully. The bases are cleverly crafted from plastic-foam circles and eggs that have been glued together. For a bit of sparkle, shiny gold ornaments form the clappers.

here's how

Using a serrated knife, trim about 1 inch off the wide end of a 6-inch-long plastic-foam egg. Repeat for a second egg. Center each egg on a 1×6-inch plastic-foam round and glue it in place with tacky crafts glue. See the photograph *below* for details. In the bottom center of each bell, carefully carve out a spot to receive a 1½-inch ornament for the clapper. Bore a small hole in the top to receive the hanging cord.

Using low-temperature hot glue and T pins or U-shaped florist's pins, cover each bell with fresh or dried moss. See the photograph *left* for details.

Tie 2½ yards of heavy satin upholstery cord into a knot and bow near the center, letting the ends hang at slightly different lengths. Hot-glue one end of the cord into the hole at the top of one of the bells. Repeat for the other bell. Remove the caps from two 1½-inch ornaments and glue them in place for the clappers.

graceful garland

Wispy snippets of cedar come together to form a soft, featherlike garland. Use short lengths of cedar or other soft greens and a light-weight twine to keep the garland soft and drapable.

here's how

Cut the cedar into 2- to 3-inch lengths. Using thin-gauge copper wire, wrap the ends of two cedar sprigs to the end of a piece of twine. Place a third sprig over the stems of the first two and wire it in place. Continue adding sprigs, wiring them in place so that the ends of the new sprigs cover the stems of the previous sprigs. See the photograph *below* for details. When the garland reaches the desired length, cut the twine and wire one last sprig in place, turning it backwards and tucking its stem under the previous sprig so that no stems are visible.

If desired, loosely wrap narrow ribbon around the garland as you drape it in place.

tooling along

An antique shovel, old rake, or any other garden tool takes on a festive feel when dressed in greens for the holidays. Use the tool instead of a wreath on a shed, garage, or the house to show your passion for gardening.

Trim two similar spruce boughs to the proper length for the base. For the shovel, we used 10-inch-long pieces, but you may need to adjust the length for the size of your tool. Wire cedar or another greenery over the spruce; then wire the ends of the cedar boughs together to form a swag.

Place the swag behind the tool at the base of the handle and wire it in place. Add a bow to the front.

see the light

A ball of greens glows magically when tiny white lights are hidden under moss and evergreen. Perch the ball in a garden pot or urn for an elegant entryway accent. At the end of the season, remove the greens and store the ball until next year, when fresh greenery can be added in minutes.

here's how

Choose a plastic-foam ball slightly larger than your container. Locate the female end of a 50-light strand of miniature white lights and embed it in the ball. Add a dab of low-temperature hot glue to secure it if needed. Wrap the lights around the ball, spacing them as evenly as possible. To hold the lights in place, use hot glue, T pins that fit between the two wires, or U-shaped florist's pins that fit over the wires. See the photograph *above* for details. Do not plug in the lights when working with them and take care not to pierce the wires. Leave the final 12 inches of the cord and the plug free.

Spread tacky crafts glue over sections of the ball and affix moss to the ball. Position the lights so they poke out from the moss surface. Use U-shaped florist's pins to further hold the moss in place, taking care not to pierce the cord with the pins.

Clip white pine or other greenery into 3- to 4-inch sprigs. Insert the greens into the ball all around, creating a full rounded shape that is lit from the inside. Place the ball in the pot or urn and plug in the lights.

SPARKLING MARTINIS The wide, shallow shape of martini glasses makes a perfect display space for pretty ornaments, floating candles, or other holiday decorations. Give a bit of sparkle to these footed pieces with a thick band of glitter. Pour decoupage medium into a shallow bowl that is slightly larger than the martini glass. Pour a deep layer of glitter into a similar bowl. Dip the rim of the glass into the decoupage medium. Lift it out and let the excess drip off. Dip the rim into the glitter, twisting the glass gently so the decoupage medium is covered with glitter. Let the glasses dry completely before using them. Do not use the glassware for serving beverages.

IN A TWINKLING
decorations

BUCKET SEATS Back each chair with a fresh look. A small galvanized bucket hanging from the upper edge of the chair holds bright kumquats but could just as easily be filled with other fruits, pinecones, greens, or ornaments. Place florist's foam in the bottom to take up some of the space and offer a cushion, then add your decorative items. To keep the contents from tumbling when the chair is moved, hot-glue the items together. Join fruits with pieces of toothpicks. Tie a ribbon around the bucket and embellish it with small ornaments or additional fruits.

The bucket used at *right* was purchased with the hanger. If similar buckets are not available in your area, create a hanger from armature wire. Drill two small holes in the back of the bucket near the rim. Hook the armature wire through the holes and shape it into an inverted V. Bend the tip of the V down to form the hanger.

STELLAR DINING Let your table shine with golden stars on the plates and linens. Sandwich star confetti between two clear glass plates for star-studded dinnerware. For one evening, simply stack the two plates together. To make the plates permanent, run a thin bead of glass glue around the outer edge of the bottom plate before putting the top plate in place. Carefully hand-wash the glued plates.

WHO'S GOT THE BUTTON? Use vintage buttons to bring winter's icy sparkle to a simple wreath. Wrap a 14-inch-diameter straw wreath form with 1½-inch-wide white grosgrain ribbon, pinning and gluing the ribbon in place to completely cover the straw. Working in concentric circles, cover all visible parts of the wreath with white buttons. For the best result, use buttons that are similar in size. Glue the buttons to the ribbon with hot glue, tacky crafts glue, or gem glue. *Note:* If vintage buttons are not available or you want a more contemporary look, substitute new buttons. Hang the wreath from a loop of wide, heavy velvet ribbon as shown *above*.

GARDEN-FRESH GARLAND Keep your garland light and airy with a ribbon sash and small clusters of boxwood and magnolia leaves. Cut the boxwood and magnolia branches to the desired length, about 8 to 10 inches for most swags. Gather the greens into small bunches and wrap the stems together with florist's tape. Cut 3-inch-wide ribbon double the length of the mantel. Tie knots in the ribbon at equidistant points. Before tightening the knots, slip the stems of the greens into them. For the ends, use slightly larger bundles of greens and multiple knots.

autumnal elegance

The natural colors and textures of fall need little to enhance their beauty. By mixing unusual materials or using them in new ways, you can give a fresh look to fall's bounty.

Combine unexpected items or use common ones in uncommon ways to enliven the goods that appear at roadside stands or farmer's markets every fall. Ivory pillar candles, oversize shimmering pearls, bright paint, and household twine add interest to gourds, pumpkins, and acorns.

gourds, acorns, and pearls

Miniature white pumpkins, acorns gathered from the yard, and large faux pearls mix it up in an intriguing table-top arrangement, *opposite*. Shape the pumpkins into a large wreath for a centerpiece or wall adornment; then create more wreaths from the acorns for candle rings. Stitch matching clusters to velvet ribbon for simple napkin ties.

Adding other textural elements to the table—nubby place mats, a runner of frayed burlap, mismatched embossed plates, heavy-stemmed glassware, and flatware with a richly aged patina— further accents the elegant shapes and natural appeal of the pumpkins, acorns, and pearls.

acorn-and-pearl candle rings

Small wreaths encircle pillar candles but also could hang in spots that need a smattering of fall embellishment. Acorns and pearls form an unusual combination in these wreaths, blending both rustic and elegant elements.

here's how

Gather the acorns, gently clean them, and let them dry for a few days. As the acorns dry, some of the caps will naturally pop off. Hot-glue them back in place, replacing a few of the nuts with ¾-inch-diameter faux pearls. See the photograph at *right* for details.

Glue the acorns to the top and sides of a 6-inch-diameter twig wreath, using a hot-glue gun. As you glue the acorns in place, check the fit of the candle to make sure the opening does not get too small. *Note:* If fresh acorns are not available, look for wooden ones at a crafts store. Paint or stain them as desired and glue the pearls to the wreath instead of attaching them to the acorn caps.

miniature pumpkin wreath

Tiny white pumpkins, which can be found with the other fall gourds, cover a straw wreath to create a centerpiece that dresses up the most casual of settings, *opposite*. Start with a moss-covered straw wreath or use tacky crafts glue to attach sheet moss to a plain straw wreath. If the wreath is to be hung, wrap heavy 16-gauge wire around it several times. Leave a loop for hanging at the back and wrap the tail of the wire around the wreath a few inches from the first wrapping. The finished wreath will be very heavy.

Working in an even pattern, position the pumpkins around the top of the wreath. It will take about 30 to 36 pumpkins to cover a 14-inch wreath. Adjust the spacing as needed, and then secure the pumpkins in place with hot glue. Place most of the pumpkins stem-side down, pressing the stems into the wreath. Place a dollop of glue in the indentations to further secure the pumpkins. For interest, leave a few pumpkins stem-side up. Repeat for the outer and inner edges of the wreath. If you plan to place a candle or another item inside the wreath, keep checking the size of the opening to make sure it's the proper size.

Squeeze hot glue into any open spaces and fill the spots with pistachios. If necessary, cluster the pistachios together. Some moss will still show between the pumpkins.

napkin tie

Repeat the candle ring's acorn-and-pearl combination with a pair of acorns tied to a napkin, replacing one of the acorn nuts with a faux pearl. As you gather the acorns, look for small twigs with pairs of acorns attached. Pick up a few extra small twigs.

Gently clean the acorns and twigs, and let them dry for a few days. For each napkin tie, pop the nut from one cap and hot-glue a ¾-inch-diameter faux pearl in place of the nut. Leave the other acorn as is. If using a twig with acorns attached, hand-tack the twig to a 12-inch length of ¾-inch-diameter velvet ribbon. If using separate twigs and acorns, sew each twig in place and glue the acorns to the twig and ribbon as if they were naturally attached.

diamond and the rough

The simplicity of this wreath's shape and structure lets the beauty of its material shine through. Four ears of Indian corn pegged together with wooden blocks showcase the rich colors and textures found only in autumn.

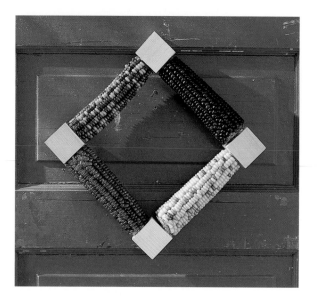

here's how

Choose four ears of Indian corn in coordinating colors and approximately the same size. Make sure the kernels are tight and the ears are solid. Using a table saw, cut the ears to exactly the same length. Drill a ¼-inch-diameter hole about ½ inch deep in the large end of each ear.

Purchase four 2-inch-square unfinished wooden blocks from a crafts store. Drill a ¼-inch-diameter hole about ½ inch deep in two adjacent sides of each block. Cut a ¼-inch-diameter dowel into eight 1-inch pieces. Use wood glue to hold a dowel in each hole. Use additional glue to hold each of the extending dowels in one of the ears of corn to form a diamond shape. See the photograph *below* for details. Drill a hole for hanging in the back of the top block. *Note*: Some kernels may fall off while you're working. Leave the spaces blank or glue the kernels back in place.

"maize" of lights

With its beautiful flecks of color, Indian corn forms the perfect base for flickering candlelight. Turning the colorful ears into candlesticks couldn't be easier. Use beeswax candles to reflect the texture of the corn.

here's how

Choose ears of corn that are solid and have tight kernels. Cut the ears to the desired length with a table saw, making sure the bottoms are perfectly flat and even. Drill a ¾-inch-deep ⅞-inch-diameter hole in the top of each ear. Glue a candle ring (available at crafts stores) into the hole with wood or crafts glue. Drill a ½-inch-deep ¼-inch-diameter hole in the large end of each ear.

Make a base for the candlestick in the same manner as the corner blocks for the wreath *above*. See the photograph *below* for details. *Note*: Ears that sit perfectly stable can have the base omitted. Never leave burning candles unattended.

pressed-leaf serving board

Make your cheeses, breads, desserts, and other treats picture perfect by serving them on a wooden tray covered with pressed dried leaves and bands of copper. An acrylic plastic sheet protects the board and leaves but does not make the tray heat-resistant. Do not use the board for serving hot items.

Purchase a rustic wooden slab with bark attached. Sand the board lightly and wipe it clean. Check the tightness of the bark; glue any loose pieces in place. Dilute medium-brown acrylic paint with an equal amount of water and brush it unevenly over the cut surface of the board. Before the paint dries or soaks into the board, wipe away most of the paint. Sand the board a second time to create an uneven, aged finish. Wipe the board clean.

Pick leaves at the peak of their color and press them in a flower press or between sheets of plain newsprint and books. If fresh leaves are not available, check crafts stores for preserved leaves or try a gourmet food store for paper French cheese leaves (made to use instead of paper doilies for serving cheeses and other foods).

When the leaves are dry, coat the backs with tacky crafts glue and smooth them onto the board. Cover the board with waxed paper and weight it with another board and heavy objects so that the leaves dry flat. Spray the board with two or more coats of satin-finish sealer.

After the sealer dries, run strips of ¼-inch-wide self-adhesive copper foiling tape in a grid over the board and leaves. Seal the tape to the board with the back of a plastic spoon.

Have an acrylic plastic sheet cut to fit the center of the board (minus the bark edges). *Note*: Because the board is in its natural shape, it may not be perfectly even and square. The acrylic plastic sheet is likely to be cut square, so it may not fit the center perfectly. Lightly clamp the acrylic plastic sheet over the board, placing a paper towel between the clamp and the sheet to prevent marks. Using a ⅟₁₆-inch drill bit and a slow speed, drill holes through the sheet and slightly into the board. Place the holes ½ inch in from the edge and space them evenly. Carefully hammer a copper nail into each hole.

To clean the board, lightly wipe it with a damp cloth and dry it with a lint-free towel. Do not soak the board.

pumpkin dressing

Make your mantel gourd-eous this year with painted and twine-wrapped pumpkins, knobby gourds, and rambling bittersweet. Swirling the pumpkins in latex paint adds a splash of sunshine brightness to fresh-from-the-patch gourds. Stick with a warm color, as shown at *right*, for a unified look or pick a palette that matches your room. For the twine-covered pumpkins, chose several fine twines, each with a slightly different color and texture. Line your mantel or table with the finished pumpkins; then add other fall findings for an eye-catching arrangement.

here's how

PAINTED PUMPKINS Decorating these small pumpkins is as simple as dip and drip. Pour satin-finish latex paint into a disposable container, such as an aluminum pan. Carefully hold the pumpkin by the stem and swirl it in the paint as shown *above*. Rolling the pumpkin will create a curving or angled shape of paint, depending on how the pumpkin is dipped. Let the excess paint drip off; then set the pumpkin on a tin can and let the remainder of the excess paint drip onto a thick layer of newspapers. Lift the pumpkin off the can several times during drying so that the paint does not stick to the can. *Note:* Use care when handling the painted pumpkins. The paint peels and scratches easily.

IT'S A WRAP Use narrow twine and hot glue to add a whole new texture to ordinary pumpkins. Squeeze a small amount of low-temperature hot glue into the dimple at the base of a pumpkin. Carefully press the end of the twine into the glue and start spiraling it around the bottom. See the photograph *above* for details. Continue adding glue and twine in concentric circles, working across the bottom and up the side.

trio of trees

Whether it hints of your hobby, displays a simple holiday motif in multiple ways, or is all done up in a single color, a tree with a theme is packed with personality.

Let your tree reflect your interests by filling it with your favorite things. Fruit ornaments show a love of the culinary arts, stars and bright colors hint of a penchant for fun, and a tree done all in white and fluff whispers its wishes in a serene way. Gather up the things closest to your heart and put them on the tree for all to see this holiday season.

chef's choice

This tree really cooks, and so would anyone who decked their fir in fruits and stars. A tree filled with fruit reflects the freshness that is important to anyone who enjoys time in the kitchen. Dozens of fruit-shaped ornaments pack the tree *opposite* much like produce packs the local marketplace. Fruit-shape ornaments are available in blown glass, beaded, frosted, sugared, and realistic varieties. Stick to one kind to keep the look unified. Add some gold stars for sparkle and a wide band of sheer ribbon for the garland. At the top, an oversized star blends in with the massive bow behind it so your eye travels throughout the tree and not just to the top. Packages below repeat the tree's colors, and the subtle patterns blend into the background.

starring attraction

Take a shine to a tree done up in bright colors and dozens of stars, *opposite*. Even the wreath on the wall and the gifts under the tree twinkle with matching colors and metallic papers. Clear glass ornaments designed for filling burst with stars and ribbons that dangle inside. Use paper punches to make the perfect small stars and cookie cutters or quilting templates as patterns for larger ones.

metaling with stardom

Foil any attempts at boredom this year with textured metal stars. Place 36-gauge aluminum tooling foil from the crafts store on a cutting mat or pad of newspapers. Using a pencil, draw the outline of a star onto the foil. Draw lines, grids, or other designs onto the stars with a sharp pencil. Press firmly so the point of the pencil makes grooves in the metal. For dots, use a stylus, a chopstick, or the eraser end of the pencil. Cut out the stars with scissors and punch a hole for hanging with a tin punch.

ribbon-of-stars garland

Wrap the tree with bands of bright ribbons bound together with paper stars. Cut corrugated paper (available at paper and art supply stores) into star shapes and make a ¼-inch-diameter hole in the center of each star. Draw three ribbons through the stars. Knot the ribbons on each side of the star using a simple overhand knot. For the most interest, vary both the widths and colors of the ribbons. The ribbons at *left* range from ¼ to 1½ inches wide.

star of the ball

Tulle fabric and purchased metallic sequins turn a plain bubble into a color-filled bauble. Cut a 4-inch square of tulle fabric. Using clear-drying fabric or gem glue, randomly attach six to eight sequins to the tulle. After the glue dries, remove the cap from a clear ornament that can be filled and use the eraser end of a pencil to push the tulle inside. Replace the cap.

the big topper

Handmade paper and glittery buttons form a topper that's oh-so-easy to make, *above*. Draw a star on large paper. Laminate the paper for strength, then cut out the star ¼ inch beyond the marked line. Make small holes with a paper punch and stitch along the line with gold braid. Sew or glue three buttons to the center of the star.

do the white thing

Whether it's done to bring back memories of a white Christmas or as a statement of elegance, an all-white tree is simply stunning, *left*. White feather boas suggest a wintry blizzard as they wind around the tree. To find boas, check crafts stores or the dress-up sections of toy departments for inexpensive small scale versions. Fill in the remaining spaces with feathery plumes, snowbirds, white ornaments, and sparkling prisms for a look that's formal but not stuffy. Wrap the presents underneath in white and frosty vellum papers, adding touches of gold and silver for sparkle.

crystal clear

Add purchased prism ornaments to any tree or make your own from chandelier dangles and beads, *near left.* Lay the beads in a pleasing order, then cut thin wire twice the bead-strand length plus two inches. Wrap one end of the wire around a jump ring. Slide the beads onto the wire, adding the prism last. Run the wire back up through the beads and attach it to the jump ring.

getting trim

Add pregathered ruffles to a purchased ornament for a flurry of frills. Place a large dot of hot glue at the top of the ornament near the cap. Press the end of the ruffle into the glue and wrap the strip around the ball, spot-gluing it in place as needed. Cut away the excess trim and glue the end in place. Add a second row in the same manner, dividing the ball into quadrants. The ruffles will overlap at the bottom.

on the fringe

Spirals of fringe, *above,* dance with delight whenever you pass by. Make a hanging loop on one end of an 18-inch piece of 12-gauge cloth-covered florist's wire. Slip two beads onto the wire. Place 2-inch-wide fringe wrong side up and run hot glue along the top edge. Press the wire into the glue, keeping the beads free. Shape the ornament around a plastic-foam cone.

HOT STUFF Hot glue gives plain satin-finish ornaments an artful raised texture, *left.* Using a low-temperature glue gun and clear glue sticks, drizzle thin lines of glue over the ornaments in random patterns.

WATCH THIS Embellishments sandwiched between the lids of two watchmaker cases create tiny see-through ornaments perfect for a miniature tree, *below.* Look for all the makings at a scrapbooking store.

Using a pop dot, adhere a metal embellishment or dimensional sticker to the inside glass of one watchmaker case lid. Top this lid with a second lid, glass-side out. Seal the lids together using double-sided tape. Starting at the top of the ornament, cover the tape with decorative trim to conceal the seam between the case tops. Shape the end of the trim into a loop for hanging. Butt the two ends, cover the joint with a small bead, and hot-glue the ends and bead in place. Add a bead or small tassel to the bottom, if desired.

IN A TWINKLING
ornaments

SNOWY SCENE Dioramas elicit a magical fascination, no matter what your age. Create wintry scenes using frames, boxes, and outdoor images. Using industrial-strength adhesive, glue the glass of a 3½×5-inch frame in place. Fit a shallow box to the frame and line the inside with the winter scene. Add bottlebrush trees and polyester quilt batting for snow, holding it all in place with industrial-strength glue. Cover the outside of the box and glue the box to the frame. Glue trim to the outside edge, then add a ribbon all around for hanging.

SWEET AS PIE Miniature tart tins form fluted frames for winter scenes snipped from old cards, *left*. Using an awl, punch a hole in the top rim of the tin. Thread ¼-inch-wide ribbon through the hole, knotting it on the inside of the tin to form a loop for hanging. Cut the card to fit inside the tin and glue it in place with tacky crafts glue. Arrange a ring of miniature artificial fruits or dried flowers around the inside of the tin, gluing it in place with industrial-strength adhesive.

PRIMARILY PRISMS Make a window or tree twinkle with a pretty prism surrounded by sparkling beads, *below*. Cut 20 inches of 24-gauge gold wire; twist one end around the tip of needle-nose pliers. Slide on a prism and enough beads to form an oval or circle around the prism. End with three to five seed beads, then wrap the wire to form the outside shape. Slide 20 seed beads onto the remaining wire and shape them into a hanging loop. Twist the end to the oval and trim away any excess wire.

CHILLING, THRILLING Let Jack (or Jill) Frost touch your tree with "ice cube" ornaments, *above*. Start with 1-inch-square glass or acrylic cubes from the floral department. Cut 12 inches of 20-gauge colored copper wire. Wrap the center of the wire around a pencil tip, creating a ¼-inch-diameter circle. Center the circle on top of the ice cube and wrap the ends of the wire around the cube as if wrapping a package. Secure the wire by wrapping it through the center circle. Wrap the ends around a skewer to curl them. Slip additional curls or a bow shape through the center, if desired.

taking stock

It just wouldn't seem like Christmas without stockings, whether they're hung by the chimney with care, laid out under the tree, used to hold special gifts, or simply incorporated as a part of your holiday decorating plan.

They're a traditional symbol of Christmas, helping spread the feeling of anticipation. When done in out-of-the-ordinary materials, stockings also become an essential part of holiday decorating. Whether they're left empty waiting for Santa's arrival or have greens and candies tucked inside throughout the season, stockings are perfect for every room.

basic stocking assembly instructions

To create the stocking shape, use a commercial stocking pattern, trace an old stocking, enlarge the outline on *page 157,* or draw your own. Be sure to add seam allowances where needed. For unlined stockings, add at least 1 inch at the top for hemming.

Cut out the stockings. For a lined stocking, cut two stocking fronts and two stocking backs. If desired, cut a layer of lightweight batting. For an unlined stockings, cut one front and one back. Be sure to flop the pattern to make fronts and backs. Add any desired embellishments before sewing.

Sew the stocking front to the back, leaving the top open. Clip the curves and turn the stocking right side out. For an unlined stocking, turn under the top seam allowance and topstitch. For a lined stocking without a cuff, sew the stocking lining in the same manner as the stocking, leaving an opening for turning. Place the stocking inside the lining with right sides facing. Sew them together along the top edge. Turn the stocking to the right side through the opening. Slip-stitch the opening closed. Topstitch around the upper edge.

To add a cuff, cut a cuff to fit the top. Cut a separate lining piece. With right sides together, sew the lining to the cuff along the bottom edge. Sew the short ends together to form a circle. Turn the cuff with wrong sides facing.

For an unlined stocking, slip the cuff inside the stocking with the wrong side of the cuff facing the wrong side of the stocking. Sew the cuff to the stocking around the upper edge. Fold the cuff over the stocking.

For a lined stocking, slip the cuff over the stocking so that the wrong side of the cuff faces the right side of the stocking and the tops are aligned. Baste the cuff to the stocking around the upper edge. Assemble the stocking as described above for the lined stocking.

the fluffy stuff

Stockings sewn from quilted fabric and chenille trim, *opposite,* bring to mind the warm, cozy feeling of Grandma's feather bed. Narrow strips of precut chenille start out flat, then fluff as you brush and wash them. Keeping the designs simple makes the trimming quick and easy and also keeps the pattern more striking. If you'd rather not draw the design freehand, trace around holiday cookie cutters, stencil templates, or shapes cut from holiday cards or stationery.

Cut the stocking pieces from pre-quilted cotton fabric as described in the general instructions. Using a water-soluble fabric marker, draw simple shapes on the stocking front. Following the manufacturer's instructions, sew chenille (we used Chenille By The Inch) along the marked lines. Fluff the chenille strips according to the manufacturer's directions.

Assemble the stocking according to the general instructions. Launder the stocking to further fluff the chenille. *Note:* Bright colors of chenille may bleed, so use a color-absorbing laundry sheet when washing the stocking.

getting to the point

Who says a stocking has to be shaped like a sock? This triangular pocket *left* is a Christmas cornucopia waiting to be filled with all sorts of holiday goodies.

Rich tone-on-tone gold fabrics and a tassel make this version elegant and sophisticated. Bright colors or funky patterns would give it a jesterlike appearance, especially if trimmed with ball fringe or jingle bells..

Enlarge the pattern on *page 156* to scale and cut out the fabric. For the front, use one fabric for the front and one for the lining. With right sides facing, sew the front cuffs together to the fold line.

Sew the stocking front to the back along the long sides from the point to the fold line, right sides facing. Clip the corners and press under the seam allowances of the back flap. Turn the stocking and cuff right side out. Turn the back flap to the inside, encasing the raw edges. Tack a cord for hanging from one upper corner to the other. Sew a tassel to the lower point and a charm to the upper point.

aged to perfection

Old stockings are expensive, hard to find, and often worn beyond repair. Get the same look with vintage fabrics or reproduction fabrics that echo your favorite era. Add ribbons for the cuffs, and you'll have stockings as good as old.

Cut a stocking front and back from vintage or reproduction fabric, low-loft cotton batting, and muslin. If desired, cut contrasting toes and appliqué them to the stocking, or piece the top of the stocking patchwork-style. Hand- or pin-baste the fabric, batting, and muslin together along the entire surface of both pieces. Machine-quilt through all layers in even stripes or along design lines. See the photograph *opposite* for details. Assemble the stocking according to the instructions for unlined stockings.

Launder the stocking to shrink the batting and create a puckered effect. Stitch a ribbon cuff to the right side of the stocking 1 inch down from the hemmed edge, as shown in the photograph.

clearly for fun

There's no hiding what's inside these stockings. Clear vinyl held together with grommets and cording makes it no secret that Christmas is merry. The vinyl sticks to itself between the grommets, keeping even the smallest of elements inside. Trim the top edge by placing felt or paper cutouts inside the pocket, or dangle beads or bangle sequins from the fold-over cuff.

To allow for the fold-over cuff, add 3 inches beyond what is the desired top edge. Cut two stocking pieces from clear vinyl yardage or a clear vinyl shower curtain. *Note:* If the vinyl has creases or wrinkles, press it between two tea towels, with the iron set on a low temperature. Take care not to use a setting that will melt the vinyl.

Fold over 1½ inches on the top edge. If desired, place the cutouts inside the fold. Fold over another 1½ inches to create a pocket. Following the manufacturer's instructions, place small grommets along the lower folded edge, spacing them evenly.

Place the two stockings wrong sides together. Mark the points for the large grommets, spacing them evenly about ¾ inch in from the outer edge and approximately 1 inch apart. Do not place grommets along the top edge.

To make installing the large grommets easier, first make holes with a paper punch. Following the manufacturer's instructions, place large grommets around the outside edges to join the two pieces. Whipstitch the edges together with cording.

Finish the upper edge by joining jingle bells or bangle sequins to the small grommets with jump rings.

stationery objects

Tiny stockings made from the prettiest of papers offer the perfect way to present gift certificates, envelopes, or flat trinkets. Enlarge or reduce the pattern on *page 157* to make more stockings for tree decorations, vignettes, or hostess gifts. The only limit is the size of your paper.

Cut a stocking back from solid red paper using deckle-edge scissors. Use regular scissors to cut a stocking front from print vellum, trimming the stocking front ³⁄₁₆ inch smaller than the back along the curved edges. Cut a cuff from red print paper.

Using a stylus, score the stocking back ³⁄₁₆ inch in from the curved edges. Clip to the scored line. Fold the deckle edge along the scored line.

Place the vellum front over the solid back, encasing the vellum edges with the folded-over back edges. Glue the deckle edges to the vellum.

Trim the cuff with additional layers of paper, bands of ribbon or paper, or beading. Glue the cuff to the stocking front.

natural beauty

Bring the rich textures and subtle colors of the outdoors into your home with centerpieces, wreaths, and garlands made from nature's best.

It's hard to beat nature as a source for beautiful materials. Wheat, grasses, pinecones, dried flowers, moss, and even nuts have been used for years as traditional crafting materials and with good reason. Each item is one of a kind and adds a pretty and handmade character to your projects. Look to crafts stores and florist's supply shops for your natural crafting materials. Avoid gathering items from public places where others will want to enjoy their beauty. Local ordinances may prohibit the gathering of materials such as fallen leaves or branches. If you do gather and dry your own materials, pick those from your own property or where the owners give you permission.

To dry the materials shown on these pages, bind the stems with rubber bands and hang them in a dark, dry, well-ventilated area. The drying time will vary with the humidity and ventilation levels. To dry pinecones, lay them out on open racks such as old screens or oven racks covered with several layers of cheesecloth.

To store projects made with natural materials, loosely wrap them in tissue paper and keep them in airtight containers that will keep bugs and rodents at bay.

dried-grass wreath and garland

Wheat, rye, oats, and dried flowers adorn a garland and wreath packed with soft green and tan colors. Each element adds a different texture, and by grouping materials rather than mixing them, you can highlight their unique textures.

here's how

FOR BOTH THE WREATH AND GARLAND: Divide dried materials, such as wheat, strawflowers, oats, rye, and baby's breath, into small bunches of like materials. Wire the bundles together, placing the heads as closely together as possible. Trim the stems to about 4 inches long.

FOR THE WREATH: Wrap the loose end of florist's paddle wire around a 12-inch straw wreath. Lay one bundle of materials over the wire and attach the bundle to the wreath form. Place the wire close to the heads, then work down toward the stems. Lay a second bundle over the first, concealing the stems of the first bundle. Wire the second bundle in place. See the photograph at *right* for details. Repeat, working in the same direction until the form is covered

FOR THE GARLAND: Cut twine to the desired length of the garland. Wrap the loose end of paddle wire around one end of the twine. Lay a bundle of dried materials over the end of the twine and wire it in place in the same manner described for the wreath. Repeat until the entire rope is covered. If the garland will be hung in a window or across a mantel, reverse the direction of the bundles at the center of the garland. If the garland will be used along a stair rail, reverse only the last bundle.

just go nuts

Buckeyes, pecans, walnuts, red pistachios, chestnuts, and other assorted nuts join up with cinnamon sticks to create a ringed topiary. A stand designed for a pillar candle forms the base of the topiary, providing the arrangement with an elegant trunk.

Brush an 18-inch-tall plastic-foam cone with tacky crafts glue, covering the entire surface except the bottom. While the glue is still wet, roll the cone in birdseed. Let the glue dry and repeat the process if needed. This creates a natural surface that blends with the nuts and softens the look of any exposed areas formed by gaps between the nuts. Hot-glue the cone directly onto the candle stand.

Starting at the bottom and working upward, hot-glue concentric rings of nuts around the cone. Fit the nuts together as tightly as possible. Create two large, flat areas by gluing cinnamon sticks around the cone. Angle the cinnamon sticks to the right for one row and to the left for the other row. Cinnamon sticks also can be used between nuts in some rows. See the photograph at *right* for details. Top the topiary with a single large nut or two buckeyes glued back to back.

pinecone candlesticks

Shed a little light on versatile pinecones by turning them into candlesticks, *opposite*. Large pinecones form the base of a candleholder, while small ones form a ring around a purchased candlestick.

here's how

FOR THE PINECONE CANDLE BASE: Paint or stain a purchased round wooden base and wooden candle cup. Drill a pilot hole in the bottom of a large pinecone. Using a countersink bit, drill through the center of the base, starting at the bottom and continuing up through the round and into the pinecone. Add a small dab of wood glue between the pinecone base and the round before tightening down the pieces with the screw.

Remove the top few scales of the pinecone to create a platform for the candle cup. Drill a pilot hole in the top of the pinecone. Drill through the candle cup and into the top of the pinecone. Add a small dab of glue between the candle cup and the pinecone before tightening down the candle cup.

FOR THE CANDLE RING: Bend 18-gauge wire into small loops, leaving a tail on each loop. Choose 10 to 12 small pinecones and hot-glue a wire loop to the bottom of each. *Note:* If the pinecones are large enough, small screw eyes can be substituted for the wire loops. Insert the screw eye into the core of the pinecone.

Paint or stain a purchased wooden candlestick. Thread the pinecones onto black elastic cord. Draw up the cord so it fits snugly around the candlestick. Arrange the pinecones in an alternating up-and-down pattern so they are tightly packed on the cord. Tie the cord in a knot and trim the ends. The pinecone ring can be

slipped off the candlestick and put onto another of a similar size.

Note: To create an aged look on the wooden pieces, hit the wood with an old screwdriver or an awl to make small holes and dents. Brush stain over the wood; then wipe it away along the high spots.

jingle
all the way

Juxtapose the rough texture of petite pinecones and the shimmer of gold jingle bells to create this charming tabletop wreath *opposite*. Look for pinecones at crafts and florist's supply stores.

Divide a 14- to 16-inch moss-covered wreath form into equal quadrants, marking off each division line with pins. At each mark, hot-glue three concentric rows of ¾-inch bells onto the wreath. Pack the bells tightly so none of the moss shows. It will take approximately 100 to 150 bells, depending on the wreath size. Remove the pins from the wreath form.

Fill in the remaining spaces with pinecones, packing them as tightly as possible. *Note:* If you prefer to hang the wreath, wrap a loop of wire around the form at one of the marked points before gluing the jingle bells in place. The bells will cover the wire.

45

moss appeal

When the colors are neutral, texture becomes all-important. Smooth glass, rough pinecones, and velvety soft moss come together as an unexpected trio that plays well as an elegant but earthy centerpiece.

Fill a clear glass compote with medium-size pinecones. Tear a piece of fresh or freeze-dried moss so it covers approximately one-third of the compote's surface. Place it over the pinecones. Look for fresh or freeze-dried moss at a florist's or crafts store. Fresh moss will last one to two weeks and needs to be misted daily and kept in a relatively humid environment. Do not dig moss from public areas. If you dig moss from your own property, use a sharp spade to cut around an area; then slide the spade under the moss to lift it from the ground underneath. Remove excess dirt. Dried moss also may be used. Look for dried moss that has a soft appearance similar to the fresh moss shown *above*.

trim a tiny tree

Petite trees, each with a distinct personality, make it easy to have a tree in every room. These pint-size tannenbaums fit easily into any spot, from a bedside table to a buffet table.

Christmas fanatics often fantasize about having a tree in every room. This year, instead of dreaming big, think small. Tabletop trees lend an air of Christmas without taking up oodles of space or decorating time. Some shown on the next few pages are created just for the holidays. Others can find a permanent place in your home after the holidays or take up residence outside if the climate is right.

baby boxwood

Formal English gardens often feature boxwoods trimmed into elaborate shapes. Bring a miniature version of one of these classic forms to a small table with a holiday version of a boxwood topiary.

Insert fresh boxwood trimmings into a 2-inch plastic-foam ball, working them into a tree shape by varying the length of the branches. See the photograph *opposite* for details.

Fill a clay pot with florist's foam, then cover the foam with moss. Use two twigs or cinnamon sticks to form the trunk of the tree, inserting one end into the tree base and the other into the pot.

Trim the branches to perfect the conical shape. Tuck slender twigs into the tree to add color and a bit of the unexpected. Top the tree with a bow.

christmas roses

Fresh roses and greens make the most elegant holiday topiary, especially when planted in a silver base. Fill a mint julep cup or similar silver container with floral foam. Insert the stem of an 8-inch-diameter ball-shaped topiary form into the base.

Using florist's picks and hot glue, cover the ball with greenery such as boxwood, juniper, or white pine. Snip the stems of miniature roses to about 1 inch; then insert them into the ball. Add a dot of hot glue to further secure the flowers. Select a second flower in the same color, such as heather for pink roses or snowberries (*Symphoricarpos*) for white roses, and hot-glue sprigs of that flower into place.

Fill the top of the vase with additional greenery or flowers to conceal the floral foam. See the photograph *opposite* for details.

tabletop tree

The term "tabletop tree" often refers to any diminutive tree, but this example *above* is true to the term. A container the size of a votive candle holder forms the base of a tree small enough to sit at a place setting on your holiday table. Make one for each setting.

Fill a votive cup or similar-size container with florist's foam. Starting at the center and fanning out in all directions to form a tree shape, insert the stems of short-needled greens, such as miniature myrtle, into the foam. Use pruners or heavy-duty shears to trim the sprigs into shape as needed. Hot-glue tiny red pepper berries or similar berries to the greens in place of ornaments.

pepper berries
and pinecones

Red is always right at Christmas, so pack this back-to-nature tree *right* with plenty of bright pepper berries. Pinecones, preserved greens, and grapevine fill in the background for the perky red dots.

Fill a woodsy container to just below the rim with floral foam, then cover the top of the foam with moss. Coat a cone-shaped topiary form with tacky crafts glue and cover it with sheet moss. Insert the stem of the topiary into the container.

Hot-glue bunches of pepper berries, slender pinecones, and preserved greenery to the topiary form, covering the moss. Starting at the top, spiral narrow grapevine garland around the tree.

dried and true

This tall, slender tree *left* may bring to mind a walk in the woods, but most of the materials are available at crafts and florist's supply stores. Use the dried materials shown here or substitute your personal favorites. A cone-shaped topiary form, complete with a "trunk," makes the crafting quick and easy.

Fill a rustic container with florist's foam, then cover the foam with moss. Coat a cone-shaped topiary form with tacky crafts glue and cover it with sheet moss. Hot-glue pinecones, lotus pods, small bundles of horsetail *(Equisetum)*, and twigs to the cone. Add gold bells for a bit of sparkle.

Insert the stem of the topiary into the base. Shape a small star from gold wire and place it at the top of the tree. Tie a multiloop bow at the bottom of the cone.

orange crush

Dried orange slices glow like stained glass, *right,* when tiny lights shine from behind. Sheer ribbon in spicy colors takes the dried fruits, pinecones, and pods from woodsy to elegant.

Slice unpeeled apples and oranges thinly and dry them in a food dehydrator or on open racks in a warm, dry place. String the dried fruits onto florist's wire. If desired, alternate the fruits with dried cherries. Tie a sheer ribbon at each end of the fruit cluster and form some into a loop. Wire the fruit strands and loops to the tree.

Dot some pinecones with glitter paint and leave others plain, then wire them to the tree. Place wild morning glory pods (also called cinch weed pods) in a warm, dry place. After the pods are dry, paint some with silver or gold metallic paint. Paint others with stripes of paint and leave some plain. Wire the pods to the tree.

Wind dried grapevine around the tree as a loose garland. If desired, tie sheer ribbon to the top of the tree and some branches.

merry rosemary

This living herb topiary *opposite* adds a warm fragrance to the kitchen or dining area. Dress it up for the holidays with dollhouse-size garlands and lightweight glass ornaments. Strip away the holiday trimmings when the season is done and keep it growing year-round.

Purchase a cone-shaped rosemary topiary and transplant it into a holiday pot. Add hand-blown glass ornaments and miniature garland or any other desired decorations.

Keep the soil moist but well drained. After the holidays, repot the rosemary into another container that provides good drainage. Place the plant in a sunny, warm location.

variations on a theme

Who says a holiday wreath has to be a perfect circle of evergreen embellished with a bow? Check out these stylish variations. They're sure to draw compliments as they add color and warmth to your home for the holidays.

Almost any type of greenery or leaves can be used to make a wreath. Large items, such as salal or evergreen branches, work best with an open wire wreath form. Smaller items, such as leaves, require a solid straw or plastic-foam wreath form.

When working with small items, gather several stems together. Attach them to the wreath form using U-shaped florist's pins. Add another bunch, pinning the leaves of the second bundle over the stems of the first. Repeat until the wreath form is completely covered.

For larger items, wire the stems of several snippets into small clusters. Attach paddle wire to one rung of the wreath form. Lay a cluster of snippets over the wreath form and wire it in place. Without breaking the wire, add a second cluster to cover the stems of the first cluster. Wire it in place. Repeat until the entire wreath form is covered.

barking up the right tree

Lichen-covered bark gathered from the ground on a walk in the woods covers a mossy wreath with subtle colors and textures, *opposite*. A wide satin ribbon adds contrast and interest to the rough surface of the wreath but blends well because the colors are similar.

here's how

Attach a wire for hanging to the back of a purchased moss-covered wreath form. Look for bark on your own property or in public areas where foraging is allowed. Do not peel bark from trees. Birch and some other barks may be available in hobby and crafts stores.

Sort the bark and set aside the most interesting pieces for the front of the wreath. Using a low-temperature glue gun, attach pieces of bark to the inside and outside edges of the wreath form.

Cover the front surface of the wreath with the remaining bark. Add a band of ribbon at the bottom of the wreath.

triple-crown winner

Three identical wreath forms, each embellished with a different kind of greenery, appear to be interlocked. In truth, they simply overlap and create an optical illusion. The finished project has powerful visual impact and is perfect for long, narrow spaces.

54

here's how

Place two 18-inch 4-wire box wreath forms about 4 inches apart on a flat surface. Lay a third form over the first two, forming a wreath chain. See the photograph *above*. Lash the wreaths together at the junctions. For details see the photograph *below*.

Clip white pine, cedar, and hemlock boughs into 3- to 4-inch snippets. *Note:* Any other trio of greenery can be used, but each wreath must have a different kind of greenery. Sort the greenery into like piles, then wire two to three snippets together to from enough bundles to cover one wreath.

Determine where each of the wreaths will intersect. Leave this spot open when filling the wreath with greens. The greenery from the wreath below it will fill this section and create the interlocking look.

Starting just above the intersection, begin wiring bundles of greenery to the top wreath. Continue around the wreath until it is covered. Leave the point of intersection open.

Cover the second wreath with a different kind of greenery, filling the open space remaining from the top wreath and leaving an open space between the second and third rings.

Add a final type of greenery to the third wreath in the same manner, filling the open space remaining from the second wreath. Add a bow if desired.

do as the romans do

An open, or Roman, wreath accents a pretty plate by leaving part of the rim exposed. Trimming away part of the wreath form is the secret. The wreath shown *opposite* is decidedly formal. Shorter greens and a more casual bow make the same wreath a perfect horseshoe shape for a country setting.

here's how

Using wire cutters, cut away two sections (one-third) of a 12-inch-diameter 4-wire box wreath form. See the photograph *below* for details. Wire pine boughs over each end to conceal the cut edges. Add a second set of boughs over the first set, concealing the wires and stems. Work around the wreath in this manner until you reach the center bottom. Conceal the center and stems with sprigs of juniper and a bow. See the photograph *opposite* for details.

To hang the wreath around a plate that is already displayed, center the wreath over the plate and mark the position of the wreath-form ends. Place a small nail at each of these points and hang the wreath from the nails.

spice is nice

Warm up your home this season with the rich, spicy colors of cinnamon, paprika, nutmeg, and mustard. Add fragrant rosemary, anise, evergreen, and fresh whole spices, and the warmth wafts through the entire house.

Pantry-fresh colors offer a break from the traditional red and green that fills most homes for the holidays. Punch up earth tones with touches of fuchsia and orange to keep the look light and bright. High-quality imitation suede adds a luxurious touch to the stockings, pillows, and table, and keeps the crafting ultraeasy with its no-fray edges. Other easy touches, such as fruit- and spice-filled decorations, help pull these rooms together in no time flat.

balancing act

When working with strong colors, use symmetry to let each of them shine through and keep the overall look from becoming a jumble of brightness. At *far right,* a square wreath is centered over a mantel covered with rosemary and arborvitae. Hurricanes filled with kumquats, candles, cherries, and spices anchor each end of the mantel display. In between, a trio of red seed balls and three soft-textured stockings add punches of color. Twin topiaries on the hearth are strung with additional fruits and spices.

Same-shaped imitation-suede stockings, each done in a different color combination, couldn't be easier to make. Cut out two stocking pieces and two cuff pieces for each stocking. Topstitch a cuff along the top edge of each stocking piece. Layer the two stocking pieces together with wrong sides facing and topstitch through all the layers, leaving the top edge open. Trim pieces with decorative-edge scissors, pinking shears, or a shaped rotary blade.

shine with color

Kumquats, star anise, whole nutmeg, cherries, and tiny pinecones hold 2-inch-wide pillar candles steady in elegant hurricane vases, *above.* Center a candle in each vase, adding a dab of floral clay to the bottom of the candle if you wish. Drop the fruits, spices, and pinecones down around the edges, coaxing them into place with chopsticks or a long skewer. Fill the vase about one-third full, using the fruits and spices to keep the candle centered.

soft wrappings

Handmade paper and sheer ribbon encircle a package that's almost too pretty to open, *left*. Wrap the package in a deep-colored plain paper. Tear fibrous art paper (available at art supply and paper goods stores) into a wide band and wind it around the package. Use double-sided tape to hold it in place. Top the band with a sheer ribbon tied in a simple bow.

For a spicy gift tag, stamp a piece of card stock with star anise. Sand one side of a star anise so it is perfectly flat. Press the anise onto a stamp pad and then onto the tag. For a raised effect, pour embossing powder over the wet ink. Shake off the excess powder and heat the embossing powder with an embossing gun, following the manufacturer's directions. Glue a larger piece of paper under the tag for a frame.

posh and plush

Jewel tones reflect the richness of spices in patchwork pillows made from luxurious imitation suede, *opposite*.

For each pillow, cut four 9-inch squares for the front and one 17-inch square for the back. Sew the four squares together using ½-inch seam allowances. Refer to the photograph for details. Trim the seams to ¼ inch. Place the pillow front over the pillow back, wrong sides facing. Topstitch around three edges, leaving a ½-inch margin. Slip a 16-inch-square pillow form into the cover and topstitch the remaining edge closed. Trim the edges with pinking shears or decorative-edge scissors.

hip to be square

Give a traditional wreath a whole new look by changing the shape. Square wreath forms are popping up at crafts stores, or cut your own from a sheet of plastic foam.

Glue rows of cinnamon sticks to the sides of a 14-inch-square wreath form. Cover the form with flat sprigs of juniper so the greens fan out and cover the outer edges. See the photograph at *right* for details. Hold the sprigs in place with U-shaped florist's pins or hot glue. Cover the juniper stems with small sprigs of boxwood, pinning or gluing them in place. Hot-glue a row of dried, fresh, or artificial red berries to the inside edge.

tasteful tabletop

Good cooking depends on a blend of flavors and textures, and so does good decorating. A gossamer tablecloth *below* provides the base for runners in deep shades of dense, soft imitation suede.

For a dash of difference, hang handmade place cards from the backs of chairs. Elevate the centerpiece by placing it on a footed tray. If a raised tray isn't available, add purchased legs to an existing tray.

To make the table runners, use decorative-edge scissors or a rotary blade to cut imitation suede to fit both the length and width of the table, allowing for a drop on each side. Each runner can fit the full length or width of the table, or two pieces can overlap at the center as shown. Cut a contrasting flatware pocket for each place setting. Position the runners on the table, then pin the flatware pockets in place on the runners. Topstitch the pockets to the runners along the side and bottom edges.

picture perfect

For a touch of nostalgia, use old photographs instead of names to guide guests to their spots at the table, *above left*. Using a photocopier or scanner and printer, copy a photograph of each guest. Use black-and-white or sepia tones to suggest the passage of time. Adjust the size of the photograph as needed and crop out all excess background. Glue the copied photograph to a piece of colored paper to form a frame, then glue the two layers to a 4×5-inch piece of handmade paper. Punch holes on the left side of the handmade paper. Thread raffia through the holes and tie a cinnamon stick to the paper. If desired, run a ribbon through the top hole and tie the card to the chair back.

star ring attraction

Simplicity often offers the most beauty, as demonstrated by the elegant napkin ring *above right*. Center a narrow sheer ribbon over a wider one and wrap the two around the napkin. Cross the ribbons in the front, leaving tails beyond the intersection. Tack the ribbons together where they meet. Using fabric, gem, or hot glue, attach a single star anise to the ribbons to cover the stitching. Tuck a sprig of holly or greens under the ribbon for a holiday look.

high style

Take a centerpiece to new heights on an elevated tray, *left* and *opposite*. Not only does the tray help the arrangement command attention, but it also gives the table a visual airiness. Arrange several spice-scented pillar candles in the tray, mixing up the colors, heights, and textures. If desired, place clear glass candle plates under the candles to protect the tray. Fill the rest of the tray with kumquats, pinecones, star anise, and greenery. *Note:* Never leave burning candles unattended.

BOWLED OVER Candles by the bowlful create a simple but elegant centerpiece, *left*, especially when the candlelight is reflected in shiny beads and baubles. Place a variety of pillar and column candles in a large bowl, using florist's clay to anchor them in place. Fill in the remaining spaces with assorted silver beads and ornaments.

GEM CLASS Add an elegant touch to a plain pillar candle with jewel-toned straight pins, sequins, and rondelle beads, *below*. Using wire cutters, shorten the shanks of the pins to approximately ½ inch. Slip a gold sequin and then a rondelle bead onto each pin. Push the pins into the candle, making sure they are evenly spaced around the candle.

To make a matching candle plate, use industrial-strength glue to attach small gem stones to the edge of a plain purchased candle plate.

IN A TWINKLING
candles

DE-LIGHT IN SLEDDING Three little votive cups find a home in a purchased wooden sled. Select three votive cups that flare out at the tops. Drill or cut holes in the sled, making sure they're large enough to receive the bottom portions of the cups. The top portion of each cup should sit above the sled. Paint the sled. Place a votive cup and candle in each opening.

BRIGHT BLOOMS
Highlight snow-white
flowers with candlelight by
placing both a blossom
and a candle in a tall, thin
cylinder vase, *right*. Place
a dot of florist's clay on the
bottom of a column
candle, then press the
candle into the vase. Cut
a single flower several
inches taller than the
candle and place it in the
vase. Add water to the
vase. Make sure the flame
of the candle is away from
the flower blossom.

**ACCESSORIZE, ACCESSORIZE,
ACCESSORIZE** Take those bracelets from
the bottom of the jewelry box and give
them new purpose as candle dressings.
It's easiest to work with stretchy bracelets,
such as the elastic cuffs and spiraled wire
bracelets shown *below*. To use bangle
bracelets, select a candle narrower than
the bracelets. Slip several bangle
bracelets over the candle and let them
stack at the base.

63

BEAD IT Dress up your candlesticks with
strands of beads for a touch of funky
elegance. Cut enough wire to loosely
wrap a candlestick or candelabra. Slip on
one bead, then twist the end of the wire
back over the bead and around itself. Fill
the wire with assorted beads, ending the
strand in the same way as the beginning.
Wind the beaded wire tightly around the
candlestick at the beginning and end and
loosely in the middle.

GATHERING

Getting together with the people we love seems so natural during the holiday season. We reflect on good times gone by and create new memories over grins and giggles. No matter what the occasion, food is at the heart of it all. Turn the pages and you'll find foods to fit fancy or casual gatherings. For fancy occasions, sit down to a Southern-style dinner or host an elegant Italian dessert buffet. For less fuss, wake up sleepy-heads with a heartland-style breakfast or organize an old-fashioned cookie exchange. And to salute the season, toast one and all with a sipper to suit any kind of party. Cheers!

TOGETHER

Coconut Bonbons (front) (recipe, page 128)
Eggnog Float (center) (recipe, page 82)
Candied Fruit Cheesecake (back) (recipe, page 102)

hanukkah

A menorah in the window, children playing dreidel games, songs handed from generation to generation, and time spent with loved ones are the traditions families share every year as they celebrate Hanukkah.

For eight nights, Jews around the world celebrate the season of light during Hanukkah. As menorahs stand glowing in windows, light prevails over darkness while an ancient miracle is remembered. This year, spread the beauty of light throughout your home with clean, bright decorations. The blue and white colors are still present, but they're softened for a sophisticated look. Paper dreidel boxes strung from the mantel and used to hold small trinkets add a lighthearted feeling. For even more fun, the word "JOY" loses a letter and becomes the well-known Yiddish expression "OY." In the rest of the house, the other classic signs of Hanukkah find a place in the decorating scheme, from gelt gift bags for every guest to creative table settings to fanciful gift wraps. Who says tradition has to be predictable? Shake things up a bit for even more fun.

dreidel, dreidel, dreidel

The dreidel song rings through homes during Hanukkah, and here, folded paper dreidels are strung to form a joyful garland, *opposite*. Others will be filled with trinkets or treats and placed as favors at the table or in the entryway as gifts for guests.

To make a dreidel box, enlarge the pattern on *page 157* to scale. Cut the dreidel and handle from card stock, cutting only on the solid lines. Transfer the Hebrew letters to the dreidel. Fill in the letter outlines with acrylic paint or cut the letters from construction paper and glue them in place.

Place the dreidel and handle right side up on a self-healing mat or piece of glass. Using a crafts knife, lightly score along the dashed lines. Fold along the scored lines to shape the dreidel into a box, folding the bottom into a point and the top into a flat lid. Fold the handle into a cube, leaving the

bottom edge open. Unfold the dreidel and handle. Place glue along the top and side flaps of the handle and refold the handle. Let the glue dry.

Place glue along the side flap of the dreidel and fold it back into a square shape. Place glue along the bottom flaps and fold the point back into place. Let the glue dry. Fold the flaps of the handle up and slide the handle through the top from the wrong side. The flaps will keep it from sliding all the way through. Glue the flaps to the underside of the top. If desired, place a small gift in the dreidel box. Fold down the top flaps and glue them to the top of the dreidel to close the box.

For the garland, thread silver cord onto a darning needle. Carefully pierce the handle with the needle and run the cord through the handle. Refer to the photograph for details. Add more dreidels, placing a knot at each side of each handle if necessary to keep them from sliding along the cord.

favorable gelt

Chocolate coins become pretty party favors when placed in organza bags, *left*. The shimmer of the coins through the shiny fabric adds sparkle to a simple table decoration.

To make each bag, use pinking shears to cut two 4×7-inch rectangles from organza. With right sides facing and using a ¼-inch seam allowance, sew along the side and bottom edges of the bag. Turn the bag right side out. Fill it with gelt or other gifts and tie it closed with ¼ yard of ribbon or cord.

playful table

Elevate the dreidel game to new heights by using its elements to decorate your dining table, *right*. Soft colors and pretty dinnerware keep the table from being garish and lend sophistication to the gelt and dreidels. For a napkin ring, tie metallic embroidery floss or cord around the napkin, leaving long tails. Tie a small dreidel to each tail. Scatter plenty of gelt around the table to add more richness and sparkle.

known presents

Every Jewish child knows there's a small gift for each night of Hanukkah. Small packages await that part of the celebration, wrapped with pretty papers and ribbons and embellished with signs of the season. The Star of David and dreidels show up as motifs throughout the decorating, and here they find a place on the packages. Cut stars from foiling metal for a bit of shimmer. Create a beaded edge around the stars with a stylus or ballpoint pen. Using a paper punch, make a hole for hanging in one of the points on each star and slide a ribbon through it.

Rubber stamping shops and office supply stores often custom-make rubber stamps at a reasonable cost. Spell out your good wishes on a stamp and apply them to fabric ribbon. Be sure to use ink designed for fabrics. Purchased rubber stamps also decorate purchased blank gift cards for a fast and easy seasonal look.

Other seasonal embellishments can be glued directly to packages. Use a hot-glue gun to attach inexpensive dreidels and gold coins (Hanukkah gelt) to the ribbon or paper.

southern ham dinner

Sit down to a holiday meal rich in Southern style and tradition. Our dinner for 12 celebrates the best of the region, from crawfish, country ham, and sweet potatoes to down-home corn bread dressing. Top it off with a moist fig cake or raisin-pecan pie, served with sweet iced tea or strong coffee.

You don't have to live in the South to appreciate the well-seasoned dishes that distinguish this congenial region. Our down-home country menu brings Southern style to your holiday table for Christmas, New Year's, or other special occasions.

Crawfish and corn combine in rich bisque to start your meal. Country ham is the perfect main course for a gathering of family and friends in the South. The slow smoking and dry curing process makes this ham a not-to-be-missed holiday delicacy.

The perfect partners for smoky ham need no introduction. Bring sweet potatoes to their full flavor with touches of orange and cane syrup. Cook up a batch of corn bread dressing studded with oysters or mushrooms. Toss steamed green beans with butter and sliced almonds.

Wrap up your holiday festivities with a choice of two Southern desserts and a steaming cup of New Orleans-style coffee. That's always a good time to move to the living room and enjoy a fireside visit.

SOUTHERN HAM DINNER

Corn and Crawfish Bisque

Country Ham with Honey-Pineapple Glaze

Corn Bread Dressing

Candied Orange Sweet Potatoes

Buttered green beans with almonds

Brown-and-serve rolls

Spiced Fig Cake
or
Bourbon Raisin-Pecan Pie

Iced tea or Café au lait

Corn Bread Dressing, Country Ham with Honey-Pineapple
Glaze, Candied Orange Sweet Potatoes (recipes, page 74)

71

BEFORE THE HOLIDAY:

up to 3 months ahead:

■ Order country ham from your butcher or a specialty source.
■ For Spiced Fig Cake, bake the cake layers but do not frost them. Place the cooled layers on a baking sheet; freeze until firm. Wrap and seal in moisture- and vapor-proof wrap or place in freezer bags; freeze for up to 3 months.

several days ahead:

■ For the Corn Bread Dressing, prepare and bake your own corn bread or a corn bread mix. Cover and store at room temperature.
■ For Corn and Crawfish Bisque, prepare the seafood stock. Cover and chill for up to 3 days.
■ For Candied Orange Sweet Potatoes, bake sweet potatoes. Cover and chill.

up to 24 hours ahead:

■ Prepare Corn and Crawfish Bisque up to the point of adding seafood. Cover and chill.
■ For Country Ham with Honey-Pineapple Glaze, begin soaking the ham.
■ Prepare Honey-Pineapple Glaze for ham. Cover and chill.
■ For Spiced Fig Cake, thaw cake layers.
■ Prepare Cream Cheese Frosting for cake. Cover and chill.
■ Prepare Spun Sugar for cake.
■ Prepare Bourbon Raisin-Pecan Pies. Cool; cover and refrigerate within 2 hours.
■ Brew iced tea. Cover and chill.

THE DAY OF YOUR CELEBRATION:

6 hours ahead:

■ Drain and begin roasting the ham.
■ Assemble Spiced Fig Cake, frosting with Cream Cheese Frosting. Cover and chill until serving time.

2 hours ahead:

■ Assemble Candied Orange Sweet Potatoes.
■ Assemble Corn Bread Dressing.
■ Beat whipping cream for pie. Cover and chill until serving time.
■ Take pie and cake out of refrigerator to come to room temperature.
■ Decorate cake with Spun Sugar and figs.
■ Spoon glaze onto ham. Bake until glaze starts to brown, spooning the glaze over the ham occasionally.

45 minutes ahead:

■ Remove ham from oven. Cover with foil to keep warm.
■ Bake Candied Orange Sweet Potatoes, Corn Bread Dressing, and brown-and-serve rolls.
■ Steam green beans and toss with butter and toasted sliced almonds; keep warm.
■ Brew coffee.
■ Add seafood to bisque and heat through.

just before serving:

■ Garnish ham with fresh fruits and parsley, if you like.
■ Dish up bisque and serve dinner.

72

73

Corn and Crawfish Bisque

Louisianans freeze the crawfish tails left over from their summer crawfish boils. You can buy frozen crawfish, shrimp, or crab.

Prep: 15 minutes   **Cook:** 25 minutes

- ⅓ cup butter
- 1 cup finely chopped onion
- ⅓ cup all-purpose flour
- 2 quarts (8 cups) seafood stock or fish stock*
- 4 cups fresh or frozen whole kernel corn
- 1 tablespoon snipped fresh thyme or
- ½ teaspoon dried thyme, crushed
- 1½ teaspoons salt
- ¼ teaspoon ground white pepper
- ¼ teaspoon cayenne pepper
- 1 pound fresh or frozen peeled, cooked crawfish tails, medium shrimp, or crabmeat, thawed
- 2 cups whipping cream, half-and-half, or light cream
- ¼ cup thinly sliced green onions or snipped fresh parsley

In a Dutch oven, melt butter over medium heat. Add onion; cook for 3 to 4 minutes or until tender.

Stir in flour; cook and stir for 2 minutes. Add seafood stock all at once. Cook and stir until bubbly; reduce heat. Simmer, uncovered, for 10 minutes, stirring often.

Stir in the corn, thyme, salt, white pepper, and cayenne pepper. Cook, uncovered, for 10 minutes more, stirring often. (If desired, cover and chill for up to 24 hours.)

Stir in the crawfish, shrimp, or crabmeat; cream; and green onions or parsley. Cook and stir about 5 minutes more or until heated through (do not boil). Makes 12 to 16 servings.

*Note: To make seafood stock, in a Dutch oven, combine 8 cups water and the shells from 8 ounces crawfish or shrimp. Bring to boiling; reduce heat. Cover and simmer for 30 minutes. Cool slightly. Strain; discard shells. Cover and chill up to 3 days.

Candied Orange Sweet Potatoes

Orange slices and cane syrup make one of the South's favorite vegetables even sweeter.

Prep: 35 minutes
Bake: 1 hour and 25 minutes

- 12 medium sweet potatoes (4 to 5 pounds total)
- 2 medium oranges, peeled (if desired), halved, and sliced
- ¼ cup butter
- ½ cup cane syrup or sorghum
- ½ cup sugar
- ½ teaspoon salt

Preheat oven to 400°F. Scrub sweet potatoes; prick with a fork. Place sweet potatoes in an ungreased 15×10×1-inch baking pan. Bake, uncovered, for 45 to 50 minutes or until tender. (If desired, cover and chill the sweet potatoes for up to 3 days.)

Reduce oven temperature to 350°F. Grease a 3-quart baking dish. Peel and cut sweet potatoes into ½-inch-thick slices. In the prepared dish, layer half of the sweet potatoes and half of the orange slices. Repeat with remaining sweet potato slices and orange slices.

In a small saucepan, melt butter over medium heat. Stir in cane syrup or sorghum, sugar, and salt. Cook and stir about 3 minutes or until the sugar is dissolved. Drizzle syrup mixture evenly over sweet potato mixture.

Bake, covered, about 40 minutes or until heated through. When serving, spoon any glaze left in the baking dish over sweet potato and orange slices. Makes 12 servings.

Country Ham with Honey-Pineapple Glaze

The pineapple is a symbol of Southern hospitality. Serving it with country ham makes folks feel especially welcome.

Prep: 25 minutes   **Soak:** 16 hours
Bake: 4½ hours   **Stand:** 20 minutes
Cool: 20 minutes

- 1 12- to 15-pound country-style ham
- 1 8-ounce can crushed pineapple
- ¼ cup honey
- ¼ cup packed brown sugar
- Assorted fresh fruits (such as pears, kumquats, persimmons, and fresh figs) (optional)
- Fresh parsley sprigs (optional)

In a deep 5-gallon pot, cover ham completely with cold water; let soak in the refrigerator for 8 hours. Remove ham; discard water. Place ham back in pot; cover completely with fresh cold water. Let soak in the refrigerator for at least 8 hours or up to 24 hours.

Preheat oven to 325°F. Drain ham and rinse with cold water. Place ham, fat side up, on a rack in a large roasting pan. Insert an oven-going meat thermometer in center of ham, making sure bulb does not touch bone. Pour 8 cups water into roasting pan.

Drain pineapple, reserving juice. Add pineapple juice to roasting pan. Cover pineapple; set aside. Cover ham; bake ham for 4 to 4½ hours or until meat thermometer registers 160°F.

Drain off pan juices; discard. Cool ham slightly (about 20 minutes). Trim skin and excess fat from ham.

For glaze, in a small mixing bowl, stir together crushed pineapple, honey, and brown sugar. Spoon glaze over the ham. Bake, uncovered, about 30 minutes more or until glaze starts to brown, spooning glaze over ham occasionally.

Cover; let stand for 20 minutes before carving ham. Transfer ham to a serving platter. If desired, garnish with fresh fruits and parsley. To serve, thinly slice ham. Makes 25 to 30 servings.

Corn Bread Dressing

For the corn bread, prepare, bake, and cool your favorite corn bread recipe or stir up a corn bread mix.

Prep: 35 minutes   **Bake:** 45 minutes

- 2 8-ounce cans oysters or 8 ounces fresh mushrooms, halved or quartered
- 1 cup chopped onion
- 1 cup sliced celery
- 3 tablespoons butter
- 8 cups crumbled dry corn bread
- 4 cups white bread cubes
- ½ cup finely snipped fresh parsley
- 1½ teaspoons poultry seasoning
- 1 teaspoon pepper
- Chicken broth

Preheat oven to 350°F. If using oysters, drain, reserving liquid. Cut any large oysters in half; set aside. Add enough chicken broth to oyster liquid to make 2¼ cups liquid. (If using mushrooms, use 2¼ cups chicken broth.) Set broth mixture aside.

In a medium saucepan, cook and stir onion, celery, and mushrooms (if using) in hot butter until tender but not brown; set aside.

In a large mixing bowl, stir together corn bread, bread cubes, parsley, poultry seasoning, and pepper. Stir in onion mixture. Add broth mixture to corn bread mixture; stir until combined. (If necessary, drizzle with additional chicken broth to moisten.) Gently stir in oysters, if using; spoon into a lightly greased 13×9×2-inch baking pan.

Bake, uncovered, about 45 minutes or until light brown. Makes 12 servings.

Country Ham with Honey-Pineapple Glaze, Candied
Orange Sweet Potatoes, Corn Bread Dressing

76

Spiced Fig Cake

Figs grow in gardens throughout the South, so fig preserves and dried figs prevail at holiday time.

Prep: 30 minutes **Bake:** 40 minutes
Cool: 10 minutes

- 2 cups all-purpose flour
- 1 teaspoon baking powder
- 1 teaspoon ground cinnamon
- 1 teaspoon ground allspice
- ½ teaspoon baking soda
- ¼ teaspoon salt
- ¼ teaspoon ground ginger
- ½ cup butter, softened
- ¼ cup cooking oil
- 1½ cups sugar
- 3 eggs
- 1 cup buttermilk or sour milk (see note, page 94)
- 1 10-ounce jar fig preserves, large pieces cut up
- 1 recipe Cream Cheese Frosting
- 1 recipe Spun Sugar (optional)
- Chopped dried figs (optional)

Preheat oven to 350°F. Grease bottoms and sides of two 9×1½-inch round baking pans. Line pan bottoms with parchment paper; grease the paper. Lightly flour pans. Set aside.

In a bowl, stir together flour, baking powder, cinnamon, allspice, baking soda, salt, and ginger; set aside.

In a large mixing bowl, beat butter with an electric mixer on medium speed for 30 seconds. Beat in oil. Add sugar; beat until combined. Add eggs, 1 at a time, beating well after each addition. Add flour mixture and buttermilk alternately to butter mixture, beating on low speed after each addition until combined. Stir in fig preserves. Pour into prepared pans, spreading evenly.

Bake for 40 to 45 minutes or until a wooden toothpick inserted near centers comes out clean. Cool in pans on wire rack for 10 minutes. Remove cakes from pans; remove parchment paper. Cool completely on wire rack. (If desired, freeze layers individually in airtight containers for up to 3 months.)

To assemble, place 1 of the cake layers on a platter; spread top with Cream Cheese Frosting. Top with remaining cake; and spread top with frosting. Cover and store frosted cake in the refrigerator for up to 24 hours.

Before serving, if desired, garnish cake with Spun Sugar and chopped figs. Makes 12 servings.

Cream Cheese Frosting: In a large mixing bowl, combine one 3-ounce package softened cream cheese, ¼ cup butter, and 1 teaspoon vanilla. Beat with an electric mixer on medium to high speed until light and fluffy. Gradually add 2 cups sifted powdered sugar, beating until smooth.

Spun Sugar: Line a baking sheet with foil; grease the foil. Set aside. In a heavy 8-inch skillet, cook ⅓ cup sugar over medium-high heat until sugar begins to melt, shaking skillet occasionally (do not stir). Once the sugar starts to melt, reduce heat to low. Cook about 5 minutes more or until all of the sugar is melted and golden, stirring as needed with a wooden spoon. Immediately drizzle caramelized sugar onto prepared baking sheet. Let stand until cool. Break into pieces.

Bourbon Raisin-Pecan Pie

There's always room for a sliver of Southern sweetness.

Prep: 40 minutes **Bake:** 50 minutes

- 1¼ cups raisins
- ⅓ cup bourbon
- 2 cups dark-colored corn syrup
- 1⅓ cups sugar
- 2 teaspoons ground cinnamon
- ½ teaspoon ground nutmeg
- ¼ teaspoon ground cloves
- ⅔ cup butter, melted
- 6 eggs, beaten
- 1¼ cups coarsely broken pecans
- 2 9-inch unbaked pastry shells
- Whipped cream (optional)

Preheat oven to 350°F. In a small saucepan, combine raisins and bourbon. Bring just to boiling over medium heat; reduce heat. Simmer, uncovered, for 2 minutes. Remove from heat; cover and let stand for 10 minutes.

For filling, in a large mixing bowl, stir together corn syrup, sugar, cinnamon, nutmeg, and cloves. Add butter and eggs; beat well. Stir in pecans and undrained raisins.

Spoon half of the filling into each pastry shell. Bake for 50 to 55 minutes or until centers are set. Cool on wire racks. (If desired, cover and refrigerate for 2 to 24 hours.) Serve with whipped cream, if desired. Makes two 9-inch pies (8 servings each).

Bourbon Raisin-Pecan Pie

Champagne Punch

toast the holidays!

Family, friends, and food. They're all worth toasting at the holidays. Gather around the punch bowl and salute shared memories and newly formed friendships. Our collection of hot and cold sippers will put your guests in a festive mood.

Champagne Punch

Bubbly champagne makes a sparkling splash in this tropical teaser.

Start to finish: 25 minutes

- 1 20-ounce can pineapple chunks (juice pack)
- 1 750-milliliter bottle dry white wine, chilled
- 1 750-milliliter bottle champagne, chilled
- ¼ cup lemon juice
- 16 cubes sugar
- 4 fresh strawberries, trimmed and quartered
- 1 fresh kiwi fruit, peeled, sliced, and quartered

Drain pineapple, reserving ¾ cup juice. In a large pitcher or punch bowl, stir together reserved pineapple juice, wine, champagne, and lemon juice.

Place a sugar cube in each glass. Pour punch over sugar cubes. Serve with small skewers of cut-up pineapple, strawberries, and kiwi fruit. Makes about 16 (4-ounce) servings.

Cranberry Honey Punch

A simple honey syrup makes a sweet base for this ruby citrus refresher.

Prep: 15 minutes **Chill:** 2 hours

- 2 cups boiling water
- ¾ cup honey
- 1 32-ounce bottle cranberry juice (4 cups)
- 2 cups orange juice
- ½ to 1 cup lemon juice
- 1 1-liter bottle ginger ale, chilled
- Ice (optional)

In a heatproof bowl, stir together water and honey; set aside to cool.

In a large punch bowl, combine honey mixture, cranberry juice, orange juice, and lemon juice. Cover and chill in refrigerator for at least 2 hours or up to 24 hours.

To serve, gradually pour ginger ale down the side of the bowl. Stir gently to combine. If desired, serve over ice. Makes 18 (6-ounce) servings.

punch points

■ To avoid diluting iced drinks with watery cubes, freeze juices, tonic, soda water, or carbonated beverages in ice cube trays.

■ To keep the fizz when adding carbonated beverages to punch, slowly pour the beverage down the side of the bowl or glass.

■ When floating citrus and other fruit slices on top of punches, stud them with whole cloves.

■ For cold punches, make an ice ring. Freeze a shallow layer of fruit juice or some of the punch in a ring mold. If you like, arrange fruit on the frozen layer and add a small amount of juice to hold it in place. Freeze until solid. To serve, unmold and float in the punch.

Punchy Sangria

Lemon and lime star in this rosy spin on the Spanish fiesta favorite.

Start to finish: 15 minutes

- 4½ cups rosé wine, chilled
- 1 12-ounce can frozen pink lemonade concentrate, thawed
- ⅓ cup lime juice
- 2 cups club soda, chilled
- 1 orange, thinly sliced
- 1 lemon, thinly sliced
- Ice

In a very large pitcher, stir together wine, lemonade concentrate, and lime juice. Slowly stir in the club soda. Add orange and lemon slices. Serve over ice. Makes about 10 (6-ounce) servings.

Cranberry Wine Sipper

For a no-alcohol version, substitute 3¼ cups white grape juice for the white Zinfandel and omit the brown sugar.

Start to finish: 25 minutes

- 2 inches stick cinnamon
- 4 whole cloves
- 1 32-ounce bottle cranberry juice (4 cups)
- ⅓ cup packed brown sugar
- 1 750-milliliter bottle white Zinfandel wine
- Fresh cranberries (optional)

For spice bag, place cinnamon and cloves in a 6-inch square of double-thickness 100-percent-cotton cheesecloth; tie with 100-percent-cotton string.

In a large saucepan, combine spice bag, cranberry juice, and brown sugar. Bring to boiling; reduce heat. Simmer, uncovered, for 5 minutes.

Remove and discard spice bag. Stir in wine; heat just until warm. To serve, ladle into mugs or heatproof cups. If desired, garnish each serving with cranberries. Makes 10 (6-ounce) servings.

Hot Gingered Cider

Ginger ale and fresh ginger pair up in this smooth soother.

Start to finish: 10 minutes

- 2 cups ginger ale
- 2 cups apple cider or apple juice
- 2 tablespoons mulling spices*
- 1 tablespoon lemon juice
- 1 1-inch piece fresh ginger, sliced

In a medium saucepan, combine ginger ale, apple cider, mulling spices, lemon juice, and fresh ginger. Cover and cook over medium-low heat for 5 to 10 minutes or until heated through (do not boil).

Strain and discard the spices. Ladle cider into mugs or heatproof cups. Makes 4 (8-ounce) servings.

*Note: If you can't find mulling spices, use a mixture of 3 inches stick cinnamon, broken, and 1 tablespoon whole cloves.

Hot Spiced White Wine

A spice bag adds flavor without adding flecks to this wine sipper.

Prep: 10 minutes   **Cook:** 15 minutes

- 4 to 6 inches stick cinnamon
- 1 teaspoon whole cloves
- 1 750-milliliter bottle dry white wine
- ¼ cup sugar
- 1 small orange, thinly sliced and halved
- 2 thin lemon slices, halved

For spice bag, place cinnamon and cloves in a 6-inch square of double-thickness 100-percent-cotton cheesecloth; tie with 100-percent-cotton string.

In a large saucepan, combine spice bag, wine, and sugar. Bring just to a simmer; reduce heat to low. Simmer, uncovered, for 15 minutes.

Remove and discard spice bag. Add citrus slices. Ladle into mugs. Makes about 6 (6-ounce) servings.

Tea 'n' Cider Wassail

Let the flavors of tea, four fruit juices, and spices brew in your slow cooker.

Prep: 15 minutes   **Cook:** 30 minutes

- 6 inches stick cinnamon, broken
- 12 whole cloves (about ½ teaspoon)
- 4 cups freshly brewed hot tea
- 1 32-ounce bottle cranberry juice (4 cups)
- 4 cups apple cider or apple juice
- 2 cups orange juice
- ¾ cup lemon juice
- 1 cup sugar
- Apple slices studded with whole cloves (optional)

For spice bag, place cinnamon and cloves in the center of a 6-inch square of double-thickness 100-percent-cotton cheesecloth; bundle up and tie with 100-percent-cotton string.

In a 4½- or 5-quart Dutch oven (or a 5-quart electric slow cooker), stir together spice bag, tea, cranberry juice, apple cider, orange juice, lemon juice, and sugar.

Bring tea mixture to boiling, stirring with a wooden spoon to dissolve sugar; reduce heat. Cover and simmer for 30 minutes. (Or cover the slow cooker; cook on low-heat setting for 5 to 6 hours or on high-heat setting for 2½ to 3 hours.)

Remove and discard spice bag. To serve, ladle wassail into a heatproof punch bowl. If desired, garnish with apple slices with cloves. Makes about 15 (8-ounce) servings.

Banana-Split Cocoa

Three great flavors—banana, caramel, and chocolate—chase away the chill!

Start to finish: 15 minutes

3	cups milk
1	large banana, cut up
⅓	cup chocolate-flavored syrup
¼	cup caramel ice cream topping
¼	teaspoon ground cinnamon
	Whipped cream (optional)
	Cinnamon sticks (optional)

In a blender or food processor, combine 1 cup of the milk, the banana, chocolate-flavored syrup, caramel ice cream topping, and ground cinnamon. Cover and blend or process until the mixture is nearly smooth.

Pour banana mixture into a medium saucepan. Add the remaining 2 cups milk. Cook and stir over medium-high heat until heated through.

To serve, pour hot mixture into mugs. If desired, garnish with whipped cream and cinnamon sticks. Makes 4 (8-ounce) servings.

82

Eggnog Float

Top off rum-laced nog with a frozen yogurt "float." Pictured on page 65.

Prep: 25 minutes   **Chill:** 4 hours

7	cups milk
1½	cups sugar
1	cup refrigerated or frozen egg product, thawed
¼	cup light-colored rum
¼	cup bourbon
1	pint vanilla frozen yogurt, softened
	Ground nutmeg (optional)

In a 4-quart Dutch oven, stir together 4 cups of the milk, the sugar, and egg product. Cook and stir over medium heat just until mixture coats a metal spoon (should take 15 to 20 minutes).

Remove from heat. Stir in remaining 3 cups milk, the rum, and bourbon. Cover and chill in the refrigerator for at least 4 hours or up to 24 hours.

To serve, pour milk mixture into glasses or a punch bowl. Add scoops of softened yogurt. Stir until desired thickness. If desired, sprinkle with nutmeg. Makes 14 (6-ounce) servings.

Spiced Cappuccino

Personalize for your palate with a cache of creamers. If you don't have an espresso maker, improvise with a drip coffeemaker.

Start to finish: 10 minutes

2	cups hot brewed espresso
½	cup flavored liquid nondairy creamer (such as amaretto, Irish crème, or French vanilla)
⅛	teaspoon ground cinnamon
1	cup vanilla ice cream
⅛	teaspoon ground cardamom

In a 2-cup glass measuring cup, stir together the hot espresso, creamer, and cinnamon. Pour into mugs. Add a small scoop of ice cream to each. Sprinkle each mug with cardamom. Makes 4 (6-ounce) servings.

Irish Cheer

Serve a crowd or just yourself. This creamy drink is as smooth as snow.

Start to finish: 10 minutes

1	750-milliliter bottle Irish cream liqueur, chilled
2	cups whole milk
1½	cups vodka, chilled
	Ice

In a large pitcher or a bowl, stir together liqueur, milk, and vodka. To serve, pour over ice. Makes about 26 (2-ounce) servings.

Note: To make a single serving, combine 2 tablespoons Irish cream liqueur, 1 tablespoon milk, and 1 tablespoon vodka. Serve over ice.

Spiced Cappuccino

Eggnog Latte

Convenient eggnog and a blender make quick work of frothy latte.

Start to finish: 10 minutes

- 2 cups dairy or canned eggnog
- 1 tablespoon light-colored rum
- 1 tablespoon bourbon
- 1 cup hot brewed espresso
- Ground nutmeg

In a heavy small saucepan, heat eggnog over medium heat until heated through (do not boil).

Stir rum and bourbon into hot espresso.

Transfer about half of the eggnog and half of the espresso mixture to a blender. Cover; blend until very frothy. Pour into mugs. Repeat with remaining eggnog and espresso mixture. Sprinkle each serving with nutmeg. Makes 5 (6-ounce) servings.

Eggnog Latte

83

heartwarming sippers

Welcome your guests in from the frosty night with mugs of steaming coffee, cocoa, or creamy drinks. Top the sippers with the little extras below.

■ Top off coffees and cocoas with swirling spoonfuls of sweetened whipped cream. Chill a medium mixing bowl and beaters of an electric mixer. To make 2 cups of whipped cream, beat 1 cup whipping cream, 2 tablespoons sugar, and 1 teaspoon vanilla or liqueur with an electric mixer on medium speed until soft peaks form.

■ Use cinnamon sticks or candy canes as stirrers for hot cocoa.

■ Instead of whipped cream, you can also top drinks with scoops of softened frozen yogurt or ice cream. Think beyond vanilla to chocolate, mocha, mint, or eggnog.

■ Sprinkle a little ground cinnamon, cardamom, or nutmeg onto whipped cream or ice cream for a finishing touch.

■ Drop marshmallows into hot cocoa to evoke cozy childhood memories.

■ When guests are arriving at different times, keep hot drinks warm in a slow cooker set on the lowest heat setting. You'll need to stir the mixture every once in a while.

lots of latkes

Latkes—potato pancakes—are traditionally made for Hanukkah because they are cooked in oil, and oil is symbolic of the holiday. Most cooks make latkes with potatoes, but why not make them with lots of different vegetables?

latkes & oil

The oil for cooking latkes represents the tiny amount of oil the Jewish people had centuries ago when they were reclaiming the Temple of Jerusalem after a war. They had barely enough sanctified oil to last one night. Miraculously, the oil lasted for eight days. Since then, followers of the Jewish faith have celebrated Hanukkah (otherwise known as the Festival of Lights) by lighting one candle every night for eight days in a special menorah (candelabrum). It's also a tradition to eat certain foods that are fried in oil, such as latkes, during Hanukkah.

Classic Potato Latkes

Serve potato latkes the traditional way—with sour cream and applesauce.

Prep: 35 minutes
Cook: 2 minutes per batch

4   medium baking potatoes (about 1½ pounds), peeled and finely shredded
3   tablespoons cooking oil
2   eggs, slightly beaten
2   cloves garlic, finely minced
½   teaspoon kosher salt
2   tablespoons cooking oil
Nondairy sour cream (optional)
Applesauce (optional)

Drain potatoes on paper towels. In a mixing bowl, combine potatoes, 3 tablespoons oil, eggs, garlic, and salt.

Using about ⅓ cup mixture for each latke, press the potato mixture into 3- to 3½-inch-wide patties, squeezing out excess liquid.

In a large skillet, heat oil over medium-high heat. Carefully slide 3 or 4 patties into 2 tablespoons hot oil. Cook over medium-high heat about 2 minutes or until latkes are golden brown, turning once. (The internal temperature should read 160°F on an instant-read thermometer). Add additional oil during cooking, as needed. If necessary, reduce heat to medium to prevent overbrowning. Drain cooked patties on paper towels; keep warm.

Repeat with remaining patties. If desired, serve latkes with sour cream and applesauce. Makes about 10 latkes.

1. Sweet Potato and
   Currant Latke
2. Classic Potato Latke
3. Zucchini Latke
4. Celery Root Latke
5. Root Vegetable Latke
(recipes, pages 84 to 87)

Root Vegetable Latkes

The roots in these latkes stem from potatoes, carrots, parsnips, turnips, and beets. Also pictured on page 85.

Prep: 40 minutes
Cook: 6 minutes per batch

- 2 medium baking potatoes (about ¾ pound), peeled and coarsely shredded* (2 cups)
- 2 medium carrots, peeled and coarsely shredded* (1 cup)
- 2 medium parsnips, peeled and coarsely shredded* (1 cup)
- 1 medium turnip, peeled and coarsely shredded* (1 cup)
- 1 medium beet, peeled, coarsely shredded,* and rinsed (⅔ cup)
- ½ cup finely chopped onion
- 1 egg, slightly beaten
- 1 teaspoon kosher salt
- ½ teaspoon ground black pepper
- 2 tablespoons cooking oil
  Nondairy sour cream (optional)
  Snipped fresh chives (optional)

Drain shredded potatoes, carrots, parsnips, turnips, and beets separately on paper towels. In a large mixing bowl, combine potatoes, carrots, parsnips, turnip, and onion. Add egg, salt, and pepper to vegetable mixture; stir to combine. Stir in beet.

Using ⅓ cup mixture for each latke, press into 3- to 3½-inch-wide patties, squeezing out excess liquid.

In a large skillet, heat oil over medium heat. Carefully slide 3 or 4 patties into hot oil. Cook over medium heat about 6 minutes or until latkes are golden brown, turning once. (The internal temperature should read 160°F on an instant-read thermometer). Add additional oil during cooking as needed. If necessary to prevent overbrowning, reduce heat to low. Drain cooked patties on paper towels; keep warm.

Repeat with remaining patties. If desired, serve with sour cream and snipped chives. Makes about 18 latkes.

*Note: Vegetables may be coarsely shredded either with a food processor or by hand.

Celery Root Latkes

This version calls for celery root, which is also known as celeriac. Pictured on page 85.

Prep: 35 minutes
Cook: 3 minutes per batch

  2   medium baking potatoes (about ¾ pound), peeled and shredded (2 cups)
  1   medium celery root (celeriac) (about ¾ pound), peeled and shredded (3 cups)
  2   tablespoons olive oil
  1   egg, slightly beaten
  2   cloves garlic, finely minced
  ¾   teaspoon kosher salt
  2   tablespoons olive oil or cooking oil
Nondairy sour cream (optional)
Applesauce (optional)

  Drain potatoes and celery root on paper towels. In a large mixing bowl, combine potatoes, celery root, 2 tablespoons olive oil, egg, garlic, and salt.

  Using ⅓ cup mixture for each latke, press into 3- to 3½-inch-wide patties, squeezing out excess liquid.

  In a large skillet, heat 2 tablespoons olive oil over medium-high heat. Carefully slide 3 or 4 patties into hot oil. Cook over medium-high heat about 3 minutes or until latkes are golden brown, turning once. (The internal temperature should read 160°F on an instant-read thermometer). Add additional oil during cooking, as needed. If necessary, reduce heat to medium to prevent overbrowning. Drain cooked patties on paper towels; keep warm.

  Repeat with remaining patties. If desired, serve latkes with sour cream and applesauce. Makes about 12 latkes.

Sweet Potato and Currant Latkes

Plump the currants in water first so they'll be juicy in the latkes. Pictured on page 85.

Prep: 35 minutes
Cook: 6 minutes per batch

  1   cup boiling water
  ¼   cup dried currants
  3   medium sweet potatoes (about 1½ pounds), peeled and finely shredded (3 cups)
  2   eggs, slightly beaten
  ⅓   cup finely chopped hazelnuts or pecans
  ¼   teaspoon ground cinnamon
  ⅛   teaspoon kosher salt
  ⅛   teaspoon ground cloves
  2   tablespoons cooking oil
Nondairy sour cream (optional)

  In a small mixing bowl, pour boiling water over currants; let stand for 5 minutes.

  Drain sweet potatoes and currants on paper towels. In a large mixing bowl, combine sweet potatoes, currants, eggs, hazelnuts, cinnamon, salt, and cloves.

  Using ⅓ cup mixture for each latke, press into 3- to 3½-inch-wide patties, squeezing out excess liquid.

  In a large skillet, heat oil over medium-high heat. Carefully slide 3 or 4 patties into hot oil. Cook over medium-high heat for 6 to 8 minutes or until latkes are golden brown, turning once. (The internal temperature should read 160°F on an instant-read thermometer). Add additional oil during cooking, as needed. If necessary, reduce heat to medium to prevent overbrowning. Drain cooked patties on paper towels; keep warm.

  Repeat with remaining patties. If desired, serve latkes with sour cream. Makes about 10 latkes.

Zucchini Latkes

It doesn't have to be Hanukkah to make latkes. Remember this recipe when your garden (or your neighbor's garden) is teeming with zucchini. Pictured on page 85.

Prep: 35 minutes
Cook: 4 minutes per batch

  2   medium zucchini (10 ounces), coarsely shredded
  1   egg, slightly beaten
  3   tablespoons matzo meal or cracker meal
  ¼   teaspoon Kosher salt
  ⅛   teaspoon ground black pepper
  2   tablespoons cooking oil
Nondairy sour cream (optional)

  Drain zucchini on paper towels. In a medium mixing bowl, combine zucchini, egg, meal, salt, and pepper.

  Using ⅓ cup mixture for each latke, press into 3- to 3½-inch-wide patties, squeezing out excess liquid.

  In a large skillet, heat oil over medium-high heat. Carefully slide 3 or 4 patties into hot oil. Cook over medium-high heat about 4 minutes or until latkes are golden brown, turning once. (The internal temperature should read 160°F on an instant-read thermometer). Add additional oil during cooking, as needed. If necessary, reduce heat to medium to prevent overbrowning. Drain cooked patties on paper towels; keep warm.

  Repeat with remaining patties. If desired, serve latkes with sour cream. Makes about 6 latkes.

Cheddar-Sausage Scones

bread & breakfast

Imagine opening your eyes this holiday and finding yourself at a cozy bed-and-breakfast inn tucked away in the snowy wooded countryside. The aromas of brewing coffee and freshly baked bread lure you to the table. That getaway comes home when you serve these satisfying breads from our coziest heartland inns.

Cheddar-Sausage Scones

Cheese and sausage make scones from Washington House Inn in Cedarburg, Wisconsin, a meal in themselves.

Prep: 20 minutes **Bake:** 12 minutes
Cool: 5 minutes

1	12-ounce package bulk pork sausage
3¼	cups all-purpose flour
½	cup sugar
2½	teaspoons baking powder
¾	cup butter
1½	cups shredded cheddar cheese (6 ounces)
¾	cup buttermilk or sour milk*

Preheat oven to 400°F. In a large skillet, cook sausage over medium-low heat until brown, breaking meat into small pieces. Drain off fat. Set aside.

In a large mixing bowl, stir together flour, sugar, and baking powder. Using a pastry blender, cut in butter until mixture resembles coarse crumbs.

Stir in sausage and cheddar cheese. Make a well in the center of the flour mixture; add buttermilk all at once. Stir just until moistened.

Turn dough out onto a lightly floured surface. Knead for 10 to 12 strokes or until dough is nearly smooth. Divide dough in half.

On a lightly floured surface, pat each half of the dough into a ¾-inch-thick circle. Using a 2½-inch floured biscuit cutter, cut out dough. On an ungreased baking sheet, arrange scones 1 inch apart.

Bake for 12 to 15 minutes or until golden. Remove from baking sheet; cool on a wire rack for 5 minutes. Serve warm. Makes 16 scones.

*Note: To make ¾ cup sour milk, place 2¼ teaspoons lemon juice or vinegar in a glass measuring cup. Add enough milk to make ¾ cup total liquid; stir. Let stand for 5 minutes.

baking scones & biscuits

Nothing says "welcome" quite like freshly baked biscuits or scones for breakfast. Try these simple tips for flaky success.

■ Stir the dry ingredients well to distribute the leavening agent.
■ Make sure butter is cold when you begin to cut it in.
■ Stir in liquid just until the dough is moistened. Overmixing after adding the liquid can make the biscuits tough.
■ Gently knead dough by folding and pressing—10 to 12 strokes should be enough to distribute the moisture.
■ Cut as many scones or biscuits as you can from a single rolling of the dough. More rolling and additional flour will make a second batch tougher than the first.

Vanilla-Walnut Cinnamon Rolls

Vanilla-Walnut Cinnamon Rolls

Don't sleep through the wake-up call at Pincushion Mountain B&B near Grand Marais, Minnesota. You won't want to miss these sticky rolls.

Prep: 45 minutes **Rise:** 1 hour
Chill: 8 hours **Stand:** 30 minutes
Bake: 25 minutes **Cool:** 10 minutes

- 1   package 2-layer-size French vanilla cake mix
- 5½ to 6 cups all-purpose flour
- 2   packages active dry yeast
- 1   teaspoon salt
- 2½ cups warm water (120°F to 130°F)
- ¼   cup butter, softened
- ¾   cup granulated sugar
- 1   tablespoon ground cinnamon
- 1⅓ cups packed brown sugar
- 1   cup butter
- 2   tablespoons light-colored corn syrup
- 1½ cups chopped walnuts

In a large mixing bowl, stir together dry cake mix, 2 cups of the flour, the yeast, and salt. Add water. Beat with an electric mixer on low speed until combined. Beat on high speed for 3 minutes, scraping side of bowl constantly.

Using a wooden spoon, stir in as much of the remaining flour as you can with a wooden spoon.

Turn dough out onto a lightly floured surface. Knead in enough of the remaining flour to make a smooth dough (about 3 minutes total; the dough will still be slightly sticky).

Shape dough into a ball. Place in a greased large bowl; turn once to grease surface. Cover; let rise in a warm place until double in size (about 1 hour).

Punch dough down. Turn dough out onto a well floured surface. Divide in half. Cover; let rest for 10 minutes.

Roll each portion to form a 16×9-inch rectangle. Spread each with half of the ¼ cup butter. In a small bowl, combine granulated sugar and cinnamon; sprinkle onto dough. Starting from a long side, roll up each dough rectangle into a spiral. Pinch to seal. Cut the dough into 1-inch-thick slices.

In a small saucepan, combine the brown sugar, the 1 cup butter, and the corn syrup. Bring to boiling. Remove from heat. Divide mixture between two 13×9×2-inch baking pans.

Sprinkle walnuts evenly into baking pans. Arrange half of the rolls, cut sides down, in each baking pan. Cover and chill in the refrigerator for at least 8 hours or up to 24 hours.

Before baking, remove from refrigerator; let stand at room temperature for 30 minutes.

Meanwhile, preheat oven to 350°F. Bake about 25 minutes or until golden. Let cool in pans on wire rack for 10 minutes. Turn out onto foil. Serve warm or cool. Cover and store at room temperature for up to 8 hours. (Or wrap, seal, label, and freeze for up to 3 months.) Makes 32 rolls.

Molasses and Rye Bread

For a rustic Swedish-inspired rye loaf, try this raisin-studded bread, laced with brown sugar and molasses. It's from Lutsen Resort on Lake Superior.

Prep: 20 minutes   **Rise:** 1½ hours
Bake: 30 minutes

    4   to 4½ cups all-purpose flour
    2   packages active dry yeast
 1½   cups water
   ⅓   cup packed brown sugar
   ¼   cup molasses
   ¼   cup shortening
 1½   teaspoons salt
    1   cup medium rye flour
 1½   cups raisins

In a large mixing bowl, stir together 2 cups of the all-purpose flour and the yeast; set aside.

In a medium saucepan, heat and stir water, brown sugar, molasses, shortening, and salt until warm (120°F to 130°F) and shortening is almost melted.

Add molasses mixture to flour mixture. Beat with an electric mixer on low to medium speed for 30 seconds. Beat on high speed for 3 minutes, scraping side of bowl constantly.

Using a wooden spoon, stir in rye flour. Stir in raisins and as much of the remaining all-purpose flour as you can.

Turn dough out onto a lightly floured surface. Knead in enough of the remaining all-purpose flour to make a moderately stiff dough that is smooth and elastic (6 to 8 minutes total).

Shape dough into a ball. Place in a greased large bowl; turn once to grease surface. Cover; let rise in a warm place until double in size (45 to 60 minutes).

Punch dough down. Turn out onto a lightly floured surface. Divide in half. Cover; let rest for 10 minutes.

Shape each portion into a loaf or a 6-inch round. Lightly grease two 8×4×2-inch loaf pans or 2 baking sheets. Place dough in prepared pans or on baking sheets. (If desired, use a sharp knife to make ¼-inch-deep cuts in a crisscross design in the tops of the round loaves.) Cover; let rise until nearly double in size (45 to 60 minutes).

Preheat oven to 350°F. Bake for 30 to 35 minutes or until bread sounds hollow when lightly tapped. Remove from pans or baking sheets; cool on a wire rack. Makes 2 loaves.

Rum-Raisin Stollen

Soak the raisins in rum or cider for this buttery treat from the Osthoff Resort on Elkhart Lake in Wisconsin.

Prep: 30 minutes   **Rise:** 1 hour
Bake: 40 minutes

   ¼   cup rum or apple juice
    1   cup raisins
 5¾   to 6¼ cups all-purpose flour
    2   packages active dry yeast
 1⅔   cups milk
   ⅔   cup butter, cut up
   ½   cup granulated sugar
    1   tablespoon vanilla sugar* or
         ½ teaspoon vanilla
   ½   teaspoon salt
   ½   cup chopped almonds
    4   teaspoons finely shredded lemon
         peel
    1   tablespoon butter, melted
    1   tablespoon granulated sugar
    1   tablespoon powdered sugar

In a small mixing bowl, pour rum or apple juice over raisins; set aside.

In a large mixing bowl, stir together 2½ cups of the flour and the yeast; set aside.

In a medium saucepan, combine milk, the ⅔ cup butter, the ½ cup granulated sugar, the vanilla sugar (if using), and salt. Heat and stir until warm (120°F to 130°F) and butter is almost melted.

Add milk mixture to the flour mixture; add vanilla (if using). Beat with an electric mixer on low to medium speed for 30 seconds. Beat on high speed for 3 minutes, scraping the side of the bowl constantly.

Drain raisins; add to dough. Using a wooden spoon, stir in almonds and lemon peel. Stir in as much of the remaining flour as you can.

Turn dough out onto a lightly floured surface. Knead in enough of the remaining flour to make a moderately soft dough that is smooth and elastic (3 to 5 minutes total).

Shape dough into a ball. Place in a greased large bowl; turn once to grease surface. Cover; let rise in a warm place until double in size (about 1 hour).

Punch dough down. Turn out onto a lightly floured surface. Divide in half. Cover and let rest for 10 minutes.

Preheat oven to 350°F. Grease 2 baking sheets; set aside. Form each portion of dough into a 9×3½-inch loaf; place on prepared baking sheets. Flatten slightly to form 10×4-inch loaves. With the side of your hand, make an indentation lengthwise down the top center of each loaf.

Bake for 40 to 45 minutes or until golden and bread sounds hollow when tapped. Remove from baking sheets; place on a wire rack.

Brush melted butter onto loaves. In a small mixing bowl, stir together the 1 tablespoon granulated sugar and the powdered sugar; sprinkle over loaves. Cool completely. Makes 2 loaves.

*Note: For vanilla sugar, split 2 vanilla beans lengthwise in half. Place in a covered container with 1 pound granulated or powdered sugar. Cover; let stand for 1 week.

Orange-Cranberry Bread (front)
and Date Pumpkin Bread (back)

Orange-Cranberry Bread

This berry-studded bread appears often on the breakfast table at the Inn at Pinewood near Eagle River, Wisconsin.

Prep: 20 minutes   **Bake:** 1 hour
Cool: 10 minutes

2	cups all-purpose flour
1	cup sugar
1½	teaspoons baking powder
½	teaspoon salt
¼	teaspoon baking soda
⅓	cup butter
1	egg
1	teaspoon finely shredded orange peel
⅔	cup orange juice
1½	cups fresh cranberries, halved
1	cup coarsely chopped walnuts

Preheat oven to 350°F. Lightly grease a 9×5×3-inch loaf pan, two 7½×3½×2-inch loaf pans, or three 5¾×3×2-inch loaf pans; set aside.

In a large mixing bowl, stir together flour, sugar, baking powder, salt, and baking soda. Using a pastry blender, cut in butter until the mixture resembles coarse crumbs.

In a medium mixing bowl, beat egg; stir in orange peel, and juice. Add to flour mixture; stir just until combined. Fold in cranberries and nuts.

Spoon the batter into the prepared pan(s). Bake until a wooden toothpick inserted in the center(s) comes out clean, allowing 60 to 70 minutes for the large loaf or 40 to 50 minutes for the small loaves.

Cool in pan(s) on wire rack for 10 minutes. Remove from pan(s). Cool completely on wire rack. Wrap and store overnight before slicing. (Or store in the refrigerator for up to 3 days.) Makes 16 servings.

Date Pumpkin Bread

Moist, spicy slices of this make-ahead loaf help guests greet the day at the Inn at Pinewood.

Prep: 25 minutes   **Bake:** 1 hour
Cool: 10 minutes

1⅔	cups all-purpose flour
1	teaspoon baking soda
½	teaspoon salt
½	teaspoon baking powder
½	teaspoon ground cinnamon
½	teaspoon ground nutmeg
¼	teaspoon ground cloves
2	eggs
1½	cups sugar
1	cup canned pumpkin
½	cup water
½	cup cooking oil
½	cup snipped pitted dates or raisins
½	cup chopped walnuts

Preheat oven to 325°F. Lightly grease a 9×5×3-inch loaf pan or three 5¾×3×2-inch loaf pans; set aside.

In a large mixing bowl, stir together the flour, baking soda, salt, baking powder, cinnamon, nutmeg, and cloves; set aside.

In a medium mixing bowl, beat eggs; stir in sugar, pumpkin, water, and oil. Add to the flour mixture; stir just until combined. Fold in dates or raisins and walnuts.

Spoon the batter into prepared pan(s). Bake until a wooden toothpick inserted in the center(s) comes out clean, allowing about 1 hour for the large loaf or about 50 minutes for the small loaves.

Cool in pan(s) on wire rack for 10 minutes. Remove from pan(s). Cool completely on wire rack. Wrap and store overnight before slicing. (Or store in the refrigerator for up to 3 days.) Makes 16 servings.

Cherry Cream Scones

Michigan's dried tart cherries add mouthwatering flavor to scones at the Terrace Inn in Petoskey.

Prep: 20 minutes   **Bake:** 20 minutes
Cool: 20 minutes

2	cups all-purpose flour
½	cup sugar
1	tablespoon baking powder
Dash	salt
½	cup butter
½	cup dried tart red cherries
2	eggs
⅓	cup half-and-half or light cream
1	teaspoon vanilla
3	tablespoons chopped almonds
2	tablespoons sugar
⅛	teaspoon ground cinnamon

Preheat oven to 400°F. Lightly grease a 10-inch springform pan or a baking sheet; set aside.

In a large mixing bowl, stir together flour, the ½ cup sugar, baking powder, and salt. Using a pastry blender, cut in butter until mixture resembles coarse crumbs. Stir in cherries.

In a small mixing bowl, beat eggs; stir in half-and-half and vanilla. Add to flour mixture; stir just until smooth.

Using your floured fingers, pat dough into prepared springform pan or into a 9-inch round on the prepared baking sheet. Sprinkle with almonds. In a small mixing bowl, combine the 2 tablespoons sugar and the cinnamon; sprinkle onto dough.

Bake until a wooden toothpick inserted in the center comes out clean, allowing 20 to 25 minutes for the springform pan or 16 to 18 minutes for the baking sheet.

Cool in pan or on baking sheet on a wire rack for 20 minutes. Remove from pan or baking sheet. Cut into wedges. Serve warm. Makes 8 scones.

Apricot-Almond Muffins

Almonds toast as they bake on top of these delightful muffins from Diana's Delights in Gaylord, Michigan.

Prep: 20 minutes **Bake:** 18 minutes
Cool: 5 minutes

  2 cups all-purpose flour
  1 tablespoon baking powder
 ½ teaspoon baking soda
 ¼ teaspoon salt
  1 egg
  1 cup buttermilk or sour milk*
 ⅔ cup packed brown sugar
 ½ cup butter or margarine, melted
 ½ teaspoon vanilla
 ¼ to ½ teaspoon almond extract
 ½ cup snipped dried apricots
 ½ cup golden raisins
 ⅓ cup sliced almonds

Preheat oven to 400°F. Lightly grease twelve 2½-inch muffin cups or line with paper bake cups; set aside.

In a large mixing bowl, stir together flour, baking powder, baking soda, and salt. Make a well in the center of the flour mixture; set aside.

In a medium mixing bowl, beat egg; stir in buttermilk, brown sugar, butter, vanilla, and almond extract. Stir in apricots and raisins. Add egg mixture all at once to flour mixture. Stir just until moistened (batter will be somewhat stiff).

Spoon the batter into prepared muffin cups, filling each two-thirds full. Sprinkle with almonds.

Bake for 18 to 20 minutes or until golden and a wooden toothpick inserted into the centers comes out clean.

Cool in muffin pan on a wire rack for 5 minutes. Remove from muffin cups. Serve warm. Makes 12 muffins.

*Note: To make 1 cup sour milk, place 1 tablespoon lemon juice or vinegar in a glass measuring cup. Add enough milk to make 1 cup total liquid; stir. Let stand for 5 minutes.

Jumbo Coffee-Cake Muffins

Jumbo is the way they make these nutty muffins at the Inn at Pinewood, but you can make the regular size at home, if you prefer.

Prep: 20 minutes **Bake:** 25 minutes
Cool: 15 minutes

    Nonstick cooking spray
1½ cups all-purpose flour
  2 teaspoons baking powder
 ¼ teaspoon baking soda
 ¼ teaspoon salt
 ¼ cup shortening
  1 egg
  1 8-ounce carton dairy sour cream
    or plain yogurt
 ½ cup granulated sugar
 ½ cup milk
 ¼ cup packed brown sugar
 ¼ cup chopped nuts
  2 tablespoons granulated sugar
  1 teaspoon ground cinnamon

Preheat oven to 350°F. Lightly coat 6 jumbo (3½-inch) muffin cups* with cooking spray or line with paper bake cups; set aside.

In a large mixing bowl, stir together flour, baking powder, baking soda, and salt. Cut in the shortening until the flour mixture is crumbly.

In a medium mixing bowl, beat egg; stir in sour cream or yogurt, ½ cup sugar, and milk. Add egg mixture to flour mixture; stir just until combined.

For filling, in a small mixing bowl, stir together brown sugar, nuts, the 2 tablespoons sugar, and cinnamon.

Spoon half of the batter into prepared muffin cups. Sprinkle with half of the nut filling. Top with remaining batter. Sprinkle remaining filling on top.

Bake about 25 minutes or until a wooden toothpick inserted into the centers comes out clean.

Cool in muffin pan on a wire rack for 15 minutes Remove from muffin cups. Serve warm. Makes 6 muffins.

*Note: For standard-size muffins, use 12 regular (2½-inch) muffin cups. Bake the muffins in a 400°F oven for 15 to 18 minutes. Cool for 5 minutes in the pan.

Raspberry Cream Muffins

At Lindgren's Bed & Breakfast in Lutsen, Minnesota, they pick wild raspberries for these muffins. For the holidays, frozen berries work well.

Prep: 15 minutes **Bake:** 18 minutes

  2 cups all-purpose flour
  1 teaspoon baking powder
 ½ teaspoon baking soda
 ¼ teaspoon salt
 ½ cup butter or margarine, softened
1¼ cups sugar
  2 eggs
  1 8-ounce carton dairy sour cream
  1 teaspoon vanilla
  1 cup fresh or frozen raspberries,
    thawed and drained
  2 tablespoons sugar
 ¼ teaspoon ground cinnamon
 ¼ teaspoon ground nutmeg

Preheat oven to 400°F. Line twenty 2½-inch muffin cups with paper bake cups; set aside.

In a medium mixing bowl, stir together flour, baking powder, baking soda, and salt; set aside.

In a large mixing bowl, beat butter with an electric mixer on medium speed for 30 seconds. Add the 1¼ cups sugar; beat with an electric mixer on medium speed until combined. Beat in eggs, sour cream, and vanilla.

Using a wooden spoon, stir the flour mixture into the beaten mixture just until moistened. Fold in raspberries. Spoon into prepared muffin cups, filling each three-fourths full.

For topping, in a small bowl, stir together the 2 tablespoons sugar, the cinnamon, and nutmeg. Sprinkle onto batter in muffin cups.

Bake for 18 to 20 minutes or until golden. Remove from muffin cups. Serve warm. Makes 20 muffins.

94

Chocolate Chip-Pumpkin Muffins

Folks at the Thorp House Inn of Fish Creek, Wisconsin, put chocolate in their pumpkin muffins. What a great idea for the holidays!

Prep: 15 minutes   **Bake:** 20 minutes

1⅔ cups all-purpose flour
1 cup sugar
1½ teaspoons ground cinnamon
1 teaspoon baking soda
¾ teaspoon ground mace
½ teaspoon salt
½ teaspoon baking powder
¼ teaspoon ground nutmeg
¼ teaspoon ground cloves
2 eggs
1 cup canned pumpkin
½ cup butter or margarine, melted
1 cup semisweet chocolate pieces (6 ounces)

Preheat oven to 350°F. Lightly grease eighteen 2½-inch muffin cups or line muffin pan with paper bake cups; set aside.

In a large mixing bowl, stir together flour, sugar, cinnamon, baking soda, mace, salt, baking powder, nutmeg, and cloves. Make a well in the center of flour mixture; set aside.

In a medium mixing bowl, beat eggs; stir in pumpkin and melted butter. Add pumpkin mixture all at once to flour mixture. Stir just until moistened (batter should be lumpy). Fold in chocolate pieces.

Spoon the batter into prepared muffin cups, filling each two-thirds full.

Bake for 20 to 25 minutes or until a wooden toothpick inserted into the centers comes out clean. Remove from muffin cups. Serve warm. Makes 18 muffins.

Chocolate Chip-Pumpkin Muffins

baking the perfect muffin

A basket of freshly baked muffins is the perfect start to the day, especially during the holidays. Here are some pointers:

■ To get nicely domed muffins without ledges on the edges, grease the muffin cups on the bottoms and only halfway up the sides.
■ After adding liquid ingredients to the flour mixture, stir just until moistened. If you stir until all of the lumps are gone, your muffins are likely to have tunnels and a tough texture.
■ Once you've mixed the batter, pop the muffins into your preheated oven right away. Batters with baking powder and baking soda need to be baked immediately so the leavening ingredient works best.
■ Muffins are done when their tops are golden and when a wooden toothpick inserted into the centers comes out clean.
■ To avoid soggy muffins, cool them in the baking pan only as long as directed in the recipe.
■ To store muffins, place them in a plastic bag, seal, and store at room temperature for up to 3 days.
■ To freeze muffins, wrap them tightly in heavy foil or place them in freezer bags and freeze for up to 3 months.
■ To reheat muffins, wrap frozen muffins in heavy foil. Heat in a 300°F oven for 12 to 15 minutes for 1¾-inch muffins or for 15 to 18 minutes for 2½-inch muffins.

delicioso desserts

Some of the world's most spectacular holiday desserts come from Italy, where tradition is revered. From panna cotta to panforte to panettone, these sweet old-world treasures will end your meal with *dolce vita!*

Chocolate Pizzelles
(recipe, page 98)

97

Panna Cotta with Cranberry Sauce
(recipe, page 98)

Chocolate Pizzelles

Think of pizzelles—made with an intricately designed iron—as thin, crisp waffle cookies. Use a hand iron or an electric one. Pictured on page 96.

Prep: 20 minutes
Bake: about 2 minutes per cookie

1½	cups hazelnuts (filberts), toasted
2¼	cups all-purpose flour
3	tablespoons unsweetened cocoa powder
1	tablespoon baking powder
3	eggs
1	cup sugar
⅓	cup butter, melted and cooled
2	teaspoons vanilla
1	recipe Chocolate Glaze

Finely chop 1 cup of the hazelnuts; set aside.

Place remaining ½ cup hazelnuts in a blender or food processor. Cover and blend or process until very fine but dry and not oily.

In a medium mixing bowl, stir together ground hazelnuts, flour, cocoa powder, and baking powder; set aside.

In a large mixing bowl, beat eggs with an electric mixer on high speed about 4 minutes or until thick and lemon colored. Reduce speed to medium; gradually beat in sugar. Beat in butter and vanilla. Add flour mixture, beating on low speed until combined.

Heat an electric pizzelle iron according to the manufacturer's directions. (Or heat a pizzelle iron on the range top over medium heat until a drop of water sizzles on the grid. Reduce heat to medium low.)

For each pizzelle, place a slightly rounded tablespoon of batter onto pizzelle grid, slightly off-center toward the back. Close lid.

Bake according to the manufacturer's directions. (For a nonelectric iron, bake about 2 minutes or until golden, turning iron once.)

Turn warm pizzelle onto a cutting board; cut in half or into quarters. Transfer pizzelles to a paper towel to cool. Repeat with remaining batter.

Dip the rounded edge of each pizzelle piece into Chocolate Glaze; dip into reserved finely chopped hazelnuts. Place on a wire rack; let stand until glaze is set. Makes 36 pizzelle halves.

Chocolate Glaze: In a small bowl, stir together 1½ cups sifted powdered sugar, 3 tablespoons unsweetened cocoa powder, and ½ teaspoon vanilla. Stir in enough milk (2 to 3 tablespoons) to make of glazing consistency.

Panna Cotta with Cranberry Sauce

Panna cotta (PAHN-nah KOH-tah) literally means "cooked cream" but also describes this eggless custard pictured on page 97.

Prep: 30 minutes   **Chill:** 4 hours

	Nonstick cooking spray
1	envelope unflavored gelatin
2	tablespoons cold water
2	tablespoons orange liqueur or orange juice
1	8-ounce carton mascarpone cheese or one 8-ounce package cream cheese, softened
1	8-ounce carton dairy sour cream
⅔	cup sugar
1	teaspoon vanilla
1	cup whipping cream
1	recipe Cranberry Sauce
	Miniature scented geranium sprigs (optional)

Lightly coat eight ½-cup molds or small cups with nonstick cooking spray; set aside.

In a small saucepan, combine gelatin, the water, and orange liqueur or juice; let stand for 5 minutes. Heat over low heat until gelatin is dissolved, stirring constantly.

In a medium mixing bowl, beat mascarpone or cream cheese with an electric mixer on medium speed until light and fluffy. Beat in sour cream, the ⅔ cup sugar, the vanilla, and gelatin mixture on low speed until smooth. Stir in whipping cream.

Pour into prepared molds or cups. Cover and chill in refrigerator about 4 hours or until firm. (If desired, store in refrigerator for up to 2 days.)

To remove panna cotta from molds, wrap a warm cloth around each mold until panna cotta is just loosened; invert onto 8 dessert plates. Or if using cups, do not unmold. Transfer Cranberry Sauce to a serving container; pass with panna cotta. If desired, garnish desserts with geranium sprigs. Makes 8 servings.

Cranberry Sauce: In a small saucepan, combine 1¾ cups fresh or frozen cranberries, ½ cup port wine or orange juice, and ⅓ cup sugar. Bring to boiling, stirring to dissolve sugar; reduce heat. Simmer, uncovered, about 5 minutes or until berries have popped and sauce is slightly thickened, stirring frequently. Stir in 2 teaspoons finely shredded orange peel. Cool to room temperature. (Or chill in the refrigerator for up to 2 days. Stir in additional orange juice if sauce is too thick.)

98

Cherry-Pine Nut Panettone

Italians share pieces of this brioche-like Christmas bread for good luck. Panettone (pan-uh-TOH-nee) is traditionally baked in a tall mold.

Prep: 30 minutes   **Rise:** 2¼ hours
Bake: 55 minutes

- ¾ cup milk
- 1 package active dry yeast
- 2¾ to 3¼ cups bread flour
- 1 egg
- ⅓ cup butter, softened
- ⅓ cup sugar
- 2 teaspoons finely shredded lemon peel
- ½ teaspoon salt
- ½ teaspoon anise seeds
- ¾ cup dried tart cherries
- ½ cup pine nuts
- ⅓ cup golden raisins
- Nonstick cooking spray
- 1 egg
- 1 tablespoon water
- 1 tablespoon pine nuts

In a small saucepan, heat milk just until lukewarm (105°F to 115°F). Pour into a large bowl. Sprinkle yeast over milk; let stand about 5 minutes or until yeast is dissolved.

Add 1½ cups of the flour, egg, butter, sugar, lemon peel, salt, and anise seeds. Beat with an electric mixer on low to medium speed for 30 seconds. Beat on high speed for 3 minutes more, scraping side of bowl constantly.

Using a wooden spoon, stir in dried cherries, the ½ cup pine nuts, the raisins, and as much of the remaining flour as you can with a wooden spoon. (The dough should be just stiff enough to knead.)

Turn dough out onto a lightly floured surface. Knead in enough of the remaining flour to make a moderately soft dough that is smooth and elastic (3 to 5 minutes total).

Shape dough into a ball. Place in a greased large bowl; turn once to grease surface. Cover; let rise in a warm place until double in size (1¼ to 1½ hours).

Coat a 7-cup panettone mold or an 8×3-inch springform pan with nonstick cooking spray; set aside.

Punch dough down; shape into a ball. Transfer dough to the prepared pan; flatten slightly to fit to shape of pan. Cover and let rise until nearly double in size (1 to 1¼ hours).

Preheat oven to 350°F. In a small mixing bowl, beat egg and water; brush onto top of loaf. Sprinkle with the 1 tablespoon pine nuts.

Bake until a wooden skewer inserted into center of bread comes out clean, allowing about 55 minutes for the panettone pan, 45 minutes for the springform pan. If necessary to prevent overbrowning, cover top loosely with foil the last 20 minutes of baking.

Cool in pan on a wire rack for 10 minutes. Remove from pan. Cool completely. Makes 1 loaf.

Bread machine directions: Following the order specified in manufacturer's directions for your bread machine, add the milk, yeast, 2¾ cups bread flour, 1 egg, butter, sugar, lemon peel, salt, and anise seeds to the pan of a 1½- or 2-pound loaf bread machine. Select dough cycle. About 10 minutes into the cycle of the bread machine (or when the machine signals), add dried cherries and the ½ cup pine nuts. When bread-machine cycle is complete, remove dough. Punch dough down. Cover and let rest for 10 minutes. On a lightly floured surface, gently knead in raisins. Shape dough into a ball. Transfer dough to prepared pan and continue rising and baking as recipe at left directs.

99

Panforte

Prep: 1 hour   **Bake:** 30 minutes

- ⅔ cup walnut halves
- ½ cup almonds
- ½ cup hazelnuts (filberts)
- 2 tablespoons pine nuts
- ⅔ cup all-purpose flour
- 3 tablespoons unsweetened cocoa powder
- 2 ounces bittersweet or semisweet chocolate, grated
- 1½ teaspoons ground cinnamon
- ¼ teaspoon ground black pepper
- ¼ teaspoon ground cloves
- ¼ teaspoon ground nutmeg
- ⅛ teaspoon salt
- ⅛ teaspoon ground cardamom
- ½ cup chopped mixed candied fruits and peels (with citron)
- ⅓ cup raisins
- 1½ teaspoons grated orange peel
- ⅔ cup honey
- ½ cup sugar
- 2 tablespoons white grape juice or water

Preheat oven to 325°F. In a baking pan, bake walnuts, almonds, and hazelnuts for 5 minutes. Add pine nuts; bake 8 minutes or until toasted. Cool.

Stir together flour, cocoa powder, chocolate, cinnamon, pepper, cloves, nutmeg, salt, and cardamom; set aside.

Grease a 10-inch springform pan; set aside. Coarsely chop ¾ cup nuts. In a large bowl, combine all nuts, fruits and peels, raisins, and orange peel. Add flour mixture; toss to coat.

In a medium saucepan, combine honey and sugar; bring to boiling, stirring to dissolve sugar. Boil gently for 3 minutes. Stir in juice. Pour over fruit mixture; stir to coat (will be thick). Press into prepared springform pan.

Bake about 30 minutes or just until firm in the center. Cool in pan on a wire rack for 15 minutes. Loosen side of pan. Cool in pan. Remove pan side. If desired, wrap and store in the refrigerator for several days before slicing. Makes 24 servings.

Cocoa Sponge Cake

Bake this cake for the trifle or serve it with whipped cream and fresh fruit.

Prep: 30 minutes   **Bake:** 20 minutes
Cool: 10 minutes

- ½ cup all-purpose flour
- 2 tablespoons unsweetened cocoa powder
- 1 teaspoon baking powder
- 2 egg yolks
- ⅔ cup sugar
- 3 tablespoons boiling water
- ½ teaspoon vanilla
- 2 egg whites

Preheat oven to 350°F. Grease an 8×8×2- or 9×9×2-inch baking pan. Line bottom of pan with waxed paper; grease paper and set aside.

In a small mixing bowl, stir together flour, cocoa powder, and baking powder; set aside.

In a medium mixing bowl, beat egg yolks and sugar with an electric mixer on high speed for 3 minutes. Reduce speed to medium; gradually beat in the boiling water and vanilla. Continue beating on high speed about 5 minutes or until the mixture thickens slightly and doubles in volume. Using a wooden spoon, fold in flour mixture.

Thoroughly wash the beaters. In another medium mixing bowl, beat egg whites until soft peaks form (peaks curl). Fold about half of the egg whites into cake batter. Fold in remaining beaten egg whites. Spread in prepared pan.

Bake for 20 to 25 minutes or until top springs back when lightly touched. Cool in pan on wire rack about 10 minutes; remove from pan. Remove waxed paper. Cool completely on wire rack. Makes 9 servings.

Sponge Cake: Prepare Cocoa Sponge Cake as directed above, except substitute 1 tablespoon all-purpose flour for the cocoa powder.

Chocolate Zabaglione Trifle

Zabaglione is a foamy Italian custard. Here it's flavored with chocolate and layered with espresso-soaked cake for a tiramisu-style dessert.

Start to finish: 30 minutes

- 1 recipe Cocoa Sponge Cake
- 4 slightly beaten egg yolks
- ⅓ cup sweet Marsala or cream sherry
- ¼ cup sugar
- ¾ cup whipping cream
- ½ cup brewed espresso or very strong coffee, cooled
- Semisweet chocolate and/or white chocolate (optional)
- Fresh mint sprigs (optional)

In the top of a double boiler, combine egg yolks, Marsala, and sugar. Place over boiling water (the upper pan should not touch the water). Beat with an electric mixer on medium speed until mixture triples in volume and temperature of mixture registers 145°F for 3½ minutes. Place the upper pan of double boiler in a larger bowl of ice water; continue beating until the zabaglione has cooled.

In a chilled large mixing bowl, beat the whipping cream with chilled beaters of an electric mixer on medium speed until soft peaks form (tips curl). Using a rubber spatula, fold the zabaglione into the whipped cream.

Spoon ½ cup of the zabaglione mixture into each of 5 dessert or parfait glasses. Using a serrated knife, cut cake into 1-inch cubes. Divide half of the cake cubes among glasses. Sprinkle each with 1 teaspoon of the espresso. Repeat layers. (If desired, cover each serving with plastic wrap. Chill in the refrigerator for up to 24 hours.)

Before serving, if desired, using a vegetable peeler, shave chocolate into curls over each serving. If desired, garnish with mint. Makes 5 servings.

100

Chocolate Zabaglione Trifle

Apple-Fig Crostata

Apples and dried figs meld to fill the sweet biscuit crust of an Italian pie.

Prep: 35 minutes **Bake:** 40 minutes
Cool: 45 minutes

- 2 cups all-purpose flour
- ⅓ cup granulated sugar
- 1½ teaspoons baking powder
- ⅓ cup butter
- 1 egg
- ⅓ cup milk
- 1 teaspoon vanilla
- 4 cups peeled, thinly sliced cooking apples (such as Jonathan)
- ⅔ cup apricot or peach preserves
- ½ cup snipped dried calimyrna (light) figs
- Milk
- Coarse sugar
- Whipped cream (optional)

102

Preheat oven to 375°F. For pastry, in a large mixing bowl, stir together flour, the ⅓ cup granulated sugar, and baking powder. Using a pastry blender, cut in butter until mixture resembles coarse crumbs. In a small mixing bowl, beat egg; stir in the ⅓ cup milk and vanilla. Add egg mixture to flour mixture; mix well. Shape into a ball.

On a lightly floured surface, knead dough gently for 10 to 12 strokes or until smooth. Remove one-third of the dough; cover and set aside. Pat remaining dough onto the bottom and up the side of a 10- or 11-inch tart pan with removable bottom (use floured hands, if necessary). Line crust with a double thickness of foil. Bake for 8 minutes. Remove foil. Bake for 4 to 5 minutes more or until light brown.

For filling, in another large mixing bowl, toss together apple slices, preserves, and figs. Spoon into the crust-lined pan.

On a lightly floured surface, roll reserved dough into a 10- or 11-inch circle. Cut into 12 wedges. Twist each wedge twice at the narrow end; arrange on apple mixture with the wide ends toward the edge. Brush dough with milk. Sprinkle with coarse sugar.

Bake, uncovered, for 40 to 45 minutes or until fruit is tender. If necessary, to prevent overbrowning, cover the tart loosely with foil for the last 5 to 10 minutes of baking.

Cool in pan on a wire rack for 45 minutes. Remove side of pan before serving. Serve warm with whipped cream, if desired. Makes 12 servings.

Candied Fruit Cheesecake

This special-occasion cheesecake is rich with the classic Italian ingredients of dried fruit, almonds, and ricotta cheese. Pictured on page 65.

Prep: 20 minutes **Stand:** 1 hour
Bake: 20 minutes **Cool:** 45 minutes
Chill: 4 hours

- ½ cup rum or orange juice
- ¼ cup diced mixed candied fruits and peels
- ¼ cup golden raisins
- 2 tablespoons sugar
- 4 teaspoons finely shredded orange peel
- 2 teaspoons finely shredded lemon peel
- 1 recipe Sponge Cake (see recipe, page 100) or one 1-layer-size white cake mix, prepared according to package directions
- 1 egg yolk
- 2 tablespoons sugar
- 2 tablespoons butter, softened
- 1 15-ounce carton ricotta cheese
- ¾ cup almonds, toasted and finely ground
- ⅓ cup sugar
- 3 tablespoons all-purpose flour
- 3 eggs
- Crème fraîche or dairy sour cream (optional)

In a small mixing bowl, stir together rum or orange juice, candied fruits and peels, raisins, 2 tablespoons sugar, orange peel, and lemon peel. Let stand for 1 hour.

Meanwhile, for crust, lightly grease the bottom and side of an 8-inch springform pan; set aside. Grate cake to make 2 cups crumbs. In a large mixing bowl, beat egg yolk. Stir in cake crumbs, 2 tablespoons sugar, and butter. Press crumb mixture onto bottom and about 1 inch up the side of the pan; set aside.

Preheat oven to 400°F. For filling, in a large mixing bowl, combine ricotta cheese, ground almonds, the ⅓ cup sugar, and the flour. Beat in the 3 eggs just until combined. In a fine sieve, drain fruit well; discard liquid. Stir fruit into ricotta cheese mixture. Spoon into crust-lined springform pan.

Bake about 20 minutes or until center appears firm.

Cool in the pan on a wire rack for 15 minutes. Loosen the crust from the side of the pan; cool for 30 minutes more. Remove side of the pan. Cool completely. Cover and chill in the refrigerator for at least 4 hours or up to 48 hours.

If desired, spread crème fraîche or sour cream onto top of cheesecake. To serve, cut cheesecake with a warm knife. Makes 8 servings.

Miniature Cannoli

While traditional cannoli are deep fried, these small cookie cones are baked before being filled with a sweetened ricotta cheese filling.

Prep: 45 minutes
Bake: 4 minutes per batch

      Nonstick cooking spray
   1 egg
  ⅓ cup all-purpose flour
  ⅓ cup sugar
   2 tablespoons butter, melted
  ½ teaspoon vanilla
  ½ cup ricotta cheese
   1 tablespoon sugar
  ½ teaspoon finely shredded orange peel
  ⅛ teaspoon ground cinnamon
  ¾ cup frozen whipped dessert topping, thawed
   1 tablespoon miniature semisweet chocolate pieces
      Finely shredded orange peel (optional)

Preheat oven to 375°F. Coat a cookie sheet with cooking spray; set aside.

In a medium mixing bowl, beat egg; stir in flour, the ⅓ cup sugar, the melted butter, and vanilla until smooth. Drop batter by teaspoonfuls, about 4 inches apart, onto prepared cookie sheet. Spread batter with back of a spoon to make 3½-inch circles.

Bake cookies, 2 at a time, about 4 minutes or until edges are light brown. Immediately loosen from cookie sheet. Carefully turn over each and roll up to form a cone. (Or wrap warm cookies around metal cannoli cones; remove cookies from cones while still warm.) Cool on a wire rack, seam sides down. Repeat with remaining batter.

For filling, in a small mixing bowl, stir together ricotta cheese, the 1 tablespoon sugar, ½ teaspoon orange peel, and cinnamon. Fold in dessert topping and chocolate pieces. Cover and chill in the refrigerator for up to 4 hours.

To serve, pipe or spoon ricotta filling into cookie cones. If desired, garnish with additional shredded orange peel. Serve immediately. Makes 16 cones.

Hazelnut Cream Cassata

Hazelnut Cream Cassata

A Sicilian specialty, this three-layer cake is filled with a hazelnut spread and topped with hazelnuts.

Prep: 30 minutes   **Bake:** 15 minutes
Cool: 10 minutes

   1 package 2-layer-size white cake mix or lemon-flavored cake mix
   1 tablespoon finely shredded lemon peel (omit if using lemon-flavored cake mix)
  ⅓ cup chocolate-hazelnut spread
  ⅓ cup ricotta cheese
 1½ cups whipping cream
   2 tablespoons sifted powdered sugar
  ⅓ cup seedless red raspberry jam
      Coarsely chopped hazelnuts (filberts), toasted

Preheat oven to 350°F. Grease and flour three 9×1½-inch round baking pans; set aside.

Prepare cake mix using the water, cooking oil, and eggs specified in the package directions. If using white cake mix, stir in the 1 tablespoon lemon peel. Divide batter among prepared pans. (If you have only two 9-inch cake pans, cover and chill one-third of the batter and bake it after the other layers are out of the pans.)

Bake about 15 minutes or until a wooden toothpick inserted near the centers comes out clean. Cool in pans on wire racks for 10 minutes. Remove cakes from pans. Cool completely on wire racks.

For filling, in a small mixing bowl, stir together chocolate-hazelnut spread and ricotta cheese.

For frosting, in a chilled large mixing bowl, beat together whipping cream and powdered sugar with chilled beaters of an electric mixer on medium speed until soft peaks form (tips curl).

To assemble, place 1 of the cake layers on a serving platter; spread top with half of the jam. Spread half of the ricotta mixture over jam. Top with another of the cake layers. Spread with remaining jam and ricotta mixture. Top with remaining cake layer. Spread frosting onto top and side of cake. Top with hazelnuts. Serve immediately or cover and chill in the refrigerator for up to 24 hours. Makes 12 servings.

104

Anise-Almond Biscotti (back) (recipe, page 106),
Nutmeg Spritz (center) (recipe, page 106), and
Cinnamon Cutouts (front)

sugar & spice cookies

The sweetest spices of the season are even sweeter when gingery, "cinnamony" holiday cookies are baking. Reach into our cookie jar for a taste of sugar and spice and everything nice. That's what these cookies are made of.

Cinnamon Cutouts

You can cut out, bake, and freeze these cookies up to a month ahead.

Prep: 30 minutes   **Chill:** 3 hours
Bake: 9 minutes per batch

- ½ cup butter, softened
- 1 cup granulated sugar
- 1½ teaspoons ground cinnamon
- 1 teaspoon baking powder
- 1 egg
- 1 egg white
- 2 cups all-purpose flour
- Coarse sugar (optional)
- Ground cinnamon (optional)

In a large mixing bowl, beat butter with an electric mixer on medium to high speed for 30 seconds. Add the granulated sugar, 1½ teaspoons cinnamon, and baking powder; beat until combined, scraping side of bowl occasionally. Beat in egg and egg white. Beat in as much of the flour as you can with the mixer. Stir in any remaining flour. Divide dough in half. Cover and chill in refrigerator about 3 hours or until firm enough to roll out. (Or chill in refrigerator up to 24 hours.)

Preheat oven to 325°F. On a lightly floured surface, roll each half of the dough to ¼-inch thickness. Using 2-inch snowflake cookie cutters or other desired shapes, cut into shapes. On an ungreased cookie sheet, arrange cutouts 1½ inches apart. If desired, sprinkle with coarse sugar and additional cinnamon.

Bake for 9 to 11 minutes or until edges are firm. Remove from cookie sheet; cool on a wire rack. Makes about 60 cookies.

Nutmeg Spritz

Grating your own whole nutmeg gives classic spritz a bolder taste. Pictured on page 104.

Prep: 30 minutes
Bake: 8 minutes per batch

1½ cups butter
1 cup granulated sugar
1 teaspoon baking powder
¼ teaspoon ground nutmeg
1 egg
1 teaspoon vanilla
3½ cups all-purpose flour
1 recipe Orange Glaze
Sanding sugar or coarse sugar
Ground nutmeg

Preheat oven to 375°F. In a large mixing bowl, beat butter with an electric mixer on medium to high speed for 30 seconds. Add the granulated sugar, baking powder, and the ¼ teaspoon nutmeg; beat until combined, scraping side of bowl occasionally. Beat in egg and vanilla. Beat in as much of the flour as you can with the mixer. Stir in remaining flour.

Push unchilled dough through a cookie press onto an ungreased cookie sheet. Sprinkle with coarse sugar and nutmeg. Bake about 8 minutes or until edges are light brown. Remove cookies from cookie sheet; cool on a wire rack.

Glaze cookies with Orange Glaze; sprinkle with sanding sugar and nutmeg. Makes 84 cookies.

Orange Glaze: In a small mixing bowl, combine 1 cup sifted powdered sugar and enough orange juice (4 to 5 teaspoons) to make an icing of glazing consistency.

106

Anise-Almond Biscotti

Anise gives a licorice-like flavor to this Italian favorite. Pictured on page 104.

Prep: 25 minutes   **Bake:** 35 minutes
Cool: 1 hour

½ cup butter, softened
¾ cup sugar
1 tablespoon baking powder
½ teaspoon salt
3 eggs
½ teaspoon vanilla
3 cups all-purpose flour
1 cup finely chopped almonds
2 tablespoons finely shredded lemon peel
2 tablespoons finely shredded orange peel
2 to 3 teaspoons anise seeds, crushed

Preheat oven to 375°F. In a large mixing bowl, beat butter with an electric mixer on medium to high speed for 30 seconds. Add sugar, baking powder, and salt; beat until combined, scraping bowl occasionally. Beat in eggs and vanilla. Beat in as much of the flour as you can. Stir in remaining flour. Stir in almonds, citrus peels, and anise seeds. Divide dough into 4 portions.

Shape each dough portion into a 5×1½-inch-long log. On an ungreased cookie sheet, place logs about 3 inches apart; flatten slightly (to about ¾-inch thickness).

Bake about 20 minutes or until a wooden toothpick inserted near centers comes out clean. Cool on cookie sheet for 1 hour.*

Preheat oven to 325°F. Using a serrated knife, cut each log into ½-inch-thick slices. On cookie sheet, arrange slices with cut sides down.

Bake for 8 minutes; turn and bake for 7 to 9 minutes more or until light brown. Remove from cookie sheet; cool on rack. Makes about 48 biscotti.

*Note: For easier slicing, after cooling logs for 1 hour, cover in plastic wrap or foil and let stand overnight at room temperature.

Rosemary Biscotti

Brew a pot of hot spiced tea to savor with herb-and-orange-scented biscotti.

Prep: 35 minutes   **Bake:** 38 minutes
Cool: 1 hour

¼ cup butter
¾ cup sugar
1 teaspoon baking powder
1 tablespoon snipped fresh rosemary or 1 teaspoon dried rosemary, crushed
½ teaspoon baking soda
¼ teaspoon salt
2 eggs
2 egg whites
2 tablespoons finely shredded orange peel
2⅔ cups all-purpose flour

Preheat oven to 375°F. In a medium mixing bowl, beat butter with an electric mixer on medium to high speed for 30 seconds. Add sugar, baking powder, rosemary, baking soda, and salt; beat until combined, scraping side of bowl occasionally. Beat in eggs, egg whites, and orange peel. Beat in as much of the flour as you can with the mixer. Stir in remaining flour. Divide dough in half.

Lightly grease a large cookie sheet. Using your lightly floured hands, shape each dough half into an 8×2½-inch-long log. On the prepared cookie sheet, place logs about 3 inches apart; flatten slightly (to about ¾-inch thickness).

Bake about 20 minutes or until a wooden toothpick inserted near centers comes out clean. Cool on cookie sheet for 1 hour.

Preheat oven to 325°F. Using a serrated knife, cut each log into ½-inch-thick slices. On cookie sheet, arrange slices with cut sides down.

Bake for 8 minutes; turn and bake about 10 minutes more or until light brown. Remove biscotti from cookie sheet; cool on wire rack. (Biscotti become crisper on cooling.) Makes about 36 biscotti.

Herb Cookies

Herb Cookies

For party tray variety, top these sweet and buttery tea cookies with different fresh herbs or herb seeds.

Prep: 20 minutes   **Freeze:** 4 hours
Bake: 12 minutes per batch

½	cup butter, softened
1	cup sugar
1	egg
1½	cups all-purpose flour
1	teaspoon baking powder
¼	teaspoon salt

Fresh herbs (such as lavender, tarragon, lemon verbena, mint, or thyme) and/or seeds (such as anise, fennel, sesame, or poppy)

In a medium mixing bowl, beat butter with an electric mixer on medium to high speed for 30 seconds. Add sugar; beat until combined, scraping side of bowl occasionally. Add egg; beat until combined. Beat in flour, baking powder, and salt. Divide in half.

Shape each dough portion into a 12-inch-long rope. Wrap and freeze about 4 hours or until firm.

Preheat oven to 325°F. Unwrap; carefully slice the frozen dough into ½-inch-thick slices. On an ungreased cookie sheet, place the slices with cut sides up. Top with desired herb or seeds; press in gently, if necessary.

Bake for 12 to 15 minutes or until edges are golden brown. Remove from cookie sheet; cool on a wire rack. Makes about 48 cookies.

Ultimate Ginger Cookies

With ground, crystallized, and fresh ginger, these treats are sure to please.

Prep: 20 minutes   **Chill:** 2 hours
Bake: 10 minutes per batch

2¼	cups all-purpose flour
2	teaspoons baking soda
2	teaspoons ground ginger
½	teaspoon salt
¾	cup butter
1	cup packed brown sugar
1	egg
¼	cup mild-flavored molasses
1	2.7-ounce jar crystallized ginger, finely chopped (½ cup)
4	teaspoons grated fresh ginger

In a medium mixing bowl, stir together flour, baking soda, ground ginger, and salt; set aside.

In a large mixing bowl, beat butter with an electric mixer on medium to high speed for 30 seconds. Add brown sugar; beat about 3 minutes or until fluffy, scraping side of bowl occasionally. Beat in egg and molasses. Gradually beat in as much of the flour mixture as you can with the mixer. Stir in remaining flour mixture. Stir in crystallized and fresh ginger.

Wrap dough in plastic wrap. Chill in the refrigerator about 2 hours or until easy to handle. (Or chill in the refrigerator up to 24 hours.) If dough becomes too stiff, let stand at room temperature for 20 to 30 minutes before using.

Preheat oven to 350°F. Shape dough into 1-inch balls. On ungreased cookie sheet, arrange balls about 2 inches apart.

Bake about 10 minutes or until brown and set. Remove from cookie sheet; cool on wire rack. Store in airtight container for up to 3 days. (Or wrap, seal, label, and freeze up to 1 month.) Makes 60 cookies.

Six-Spice Cutouts

Let these shaped cookies show you how spice flavors can blend sweetly.

Prep: 30 minutes   **Chill:** 2 hours
Bake: 5 minutes per batch

2½	cups all-purpose flour
1	teaspoon baking powder
1	tablespoon ground cardamom
2	teaspoons ground cinnamon
½	teaspoon ground ginger
½	teaspoon ground nutmeg
½	teaspoon ground allspice
¼	teaspoon salt
¼	teaspoon ground cloves
1	cup butter, softened
1½	cups sugar
1	large egg
1	tablespoon molasses
	Powdered Sugar Icing (recipe, opposite page) (optional)

In a medium mixing bowl, stir together flour, baking powder, cardamom, cinnamon, ginger, nutmeg, allspice, salt, and cloves; set aside.

In a large mixing bowl, beat butter with an electric mixer on medium to high speed for 30 seconds. Add sugar; beat about 3 minutes or until fluffy, scraping side of bowl occasionally. Beat in egg and molasses. Gradually beat in as much of the flour mixture as you can with the mixer. Stir in remaining flour mixture.

Divide dough into 4 portions; shape into thick disks. Wrap tightly in plastic wrap. Chill in the refrigerator about 2 hours or until easy to handle. (Or chill in refrigerator up to 24 hours.)

Preheat oven to 400°F. On a lightly floured surface, roll 1 portion of dough to ⅛-inch thickness (keep remaining dough refrigerated). Using a 3-inch cookie cutter, cut dough into shapes. On ungreased cookie sheet, arrange cookies about 1 inch apart.

Bake for 5 to 7 minutes or until edges are firm and beginning to brown. Cool on cookie sheet for 1 minute. Remove from cookie sheet; cool on wire rack. If desired, decorate with icing. Makes about 60 cookies.

Eggnog Thumbprints

Fill cookies with rum-flavored filling, then dust with nutmeg.

Prep: 45 minutes   **Chill:** 1 hour
Bake: 10 minutes per batch

⅔	cup butter, softened
½	cup sugar
⅛	teaspoon ground nutmeg
2	egg yolks
1	teaspoon vanilla
1½	cups all-purpose flour
2	egg whites, slightly beaten
1	cup finely chopped walnuts
1	recipe Eggnog Filling
	Ground nutmeg

In a medium mixing bowl, beat butter with an electric mixer on medium to high speed for 30 seconds. Add sugar and ⅛ teaspoon nutmeg; beat until combined, scraping side of bowl occasionally. Beat in egg yolks and vanilla. Gradually beat in as much of the flour as you can with the mixer. Stir in any remaining flour. (If necessary, cover and chill dough in the refrigerator about 1 hour or until easy to handle.)

Preheat oven to 375°F. Lightly grease cookie sheet; set aside. Shape dough into 1-inch balls. Roll balls in egg whites; roll in walnuts to coat. On prepared cookie sheet, arrange balls 1 inch apart. Press your thumb into the center of each ball.

Bake for 10 to 12 minutes or until edges are light brown. Remove from cookie sheet; cool on wire rack.

Spoon or pipe about ½ teaspoon of the Eggnog Filling into the center of each cookie. Sprinkle with nutmeg. Makes about 40 cookies.

Eggnog Filling: In a small mixing bowl, beat ¼ cup butter with an electric mixer on medium speed until softened. Add 1 cup sifted powdered sugar; beat until fluffy. Beat in 1 teaspoon rum or ¼ teaspoon rum extract and enough milk (1 to 2 teaspoons) to make a filling of spreading consistency.

Quilt-Block Cookies

Give these sandwich cookies a "stitched" look by piping with icing.

Prep: 35 minutes   **Chill:** 2 hours
Bake: 6 minutes per batch

- ½   cup butter
- ½   cup packed brown sugar
- ½   teaspoon baking soda
- ½   teaspoon ground cardamom or
      1 teaspoon ground cinnamon
- 1   egg
- ⅓   cup honey
- 1   teaspoon vanilla
- 1   cup all-purpose flour
- 1   cup whole wheat flour
- 1   recipe Cherry Filling
- 1   recipe Powdered Sugar Icing

In a large mixing bowl, beat butter with an electric mixer on medium speed for 30 seconds. Add brown sugar, baking soda, and cardamom; beat until combined, scraping side of bowl occasionally. Beat in egg, honey, and vanilla. Beat in all-purpose flour. Stir in whole wheat flour. Divide dough in half. Cover and chill in the refrigerator about 2 hours or until dough is easy to handle.

Preheat oven to 375°F. On a lightly floured surface, roll each half of the dough to a 13×11-inch rectangle. Using a fluted pastry wheel, trim to a 12½ ×10-inch rectangle; cut into twenty 2½-inch squares.

On an ungreased cookie sheet, arrange half of the squares 1 inch apart. Spread about 1 teaspoon of the Cherry Filling in the center of each square.

Using 1-inch star-, heart-, and/or tree-shaped cookie cutters, cut out and remove a shape from the center of each of the remaining squares. Place a square with a cutout on top of each filled square; press edges to seal. Reroll dough trimmings; repeat.

Bake for 6 to 8 minutes or until edges are light brown. Remove from cookie sheet; cool on a wire rack.

Quilt-Block Cookies

Pipe Powdered Sugar Icing in lines along the edges of cookies to look like stitching. Makes about 24 cookies.

Cherry Filling: In a small saucepan, combine 1 cup dried tart red cherries, ½ cup cherry blend drink or apple juice, and 1 tablespoon lemon juice. Bring just to boiling; reduce heat. Simmer, uncovered, about 10 minutes or until cherries are tender and most of the liquid is absorbed, stirring occasionally. Remove from heat; stir in 2 tablespoons granulated sugar. Cool slightly. Transfer mixture to a food processor or blender. Cover and process or blend until a paste forms. Cool completely.

Powdered Sugar Icing: In a small mixing bowl, combine 1 cup sifted powdered sugar, ¼ teaspoon vanilla, and enough milk (2 to 4 teaspoons) to make an icing of piping consistency.

109

TRIM THE COOKIE TREE: Frost tree-shaped cookies, *left,* in shades of green by adding green food coloring to Powdered Sugar Icing (see recipe, page 109). Tint the whole batch, then reserve some to add a little more green for a darker shade. Frost the cookies in the lighter shade, then use a paint brush to apply the darker green. When the frosting is set, decorate the tree by piping on balls of red decorating gel.

FROST FOREST CUPCAKES: Jack Frost would be delighted with these frosty cakes *below.* Top cupcakes with canned vanilla frosting. Brush light-colored corn syrup onto fresh cranberries and sprigs of rosemary. Sprinkle with coarse sugar (the syrup makes the sugar stick). Arrange berries and branches on top of the snow-capped cakes and serve.

IN A TWINKLING
red & green garnishes

FREEZE FRUITY ICE CUBES: Say "Cheers!" with red and green ice cubes. Simply arrange cut-up strawberries or raspberries and cut-up seedless green grapes or kiwi fruit in the sections of an ice cube tray. Add water or sparkling water and freeze. Bring the cubes out at party time to chill wine, punch, or soft drinks.

PEP UP DIPS: To garnish party dips, use red and green sweet pepper cutouts to make holly berries and leaves, *above.* Halve and seed a green and a red pepper. Using a wide section of each color, carefully cut out leaf and berry shapes with a paring knife or kitchen scissors. Arrange the holly shapes on the dip.

STIR UP A SIPPER: Red- and green-striped candy canes serve triple duty in a frothy glass of eggnog, *above,* or hot chocolate. The candy canes add holiday cheer, act as handy stirrers, and impart a refreshing minty flavor to drinks.

SPARKLE WITH POMEGRANATE: Discover a holiday treasure in pomegranate seeds and fresh herbs. Just open up a fresh pomegranate and sprinkle its sparkling red gems onto desserts or salads. Add a little fresh mint and you've got a 60-second garnish that'll remind you of the crown jewels.

new year's celebration

Welcome guests to a party that reflects your mood for the season. A New Year's table filled with sparkle, bright colors, and retro decorations leaves no doubt that fun is in store.

Cheers! It's time to pull out all the stops and celebrate. While some may prefer to use New Year's Eve for looking back on the previous year, we look back even further to a time when silver trees, Miami-bright colors, mirrored balls, and top hats were in vogue. Put some old-fashioned rock and roll on the stereo and party away.

new year's reflections

There's no doubt that fun and funky is the theme for a New Year's celebration done up with bright colors and loads of sparkle. A vintage aluminum tree is the inspiration for the mirrored centerpiece and retro-style hat and horn ornaments, *opposite*. Flamingo-pink linens provide a strong background for all the sparkle and fit well with the rest of the fanciful designs. If bright linens aren't available in the size or color you need, use fabric dye to tint 100-percent-cotton linens the shade you desire. For extra-bold colors, a double dose of dye or more than one trip through the dye bath may be needed.

hats off!

Top a tree with a festive hat. Party horns sprouting from the top hat *left* are sure to bring a smile to everyone's face. Once you've topped the tree, tie additional horns to the branches with silver ribbon.

FOR THE HORNS: Cut 8-inch lengths of iridescent cellophane and white tissue paper for each horn. Layer the iridescent cellophane and tissue paper together and fold the strips in half crosswise. Working from the open long edge, cut down toward the fold to form fringe. Cut the fringe into smaller segments and tape the segments inside the horns. Spiral shiny metallic wired ribbon around each horn, spot-gluing it in place as you work. Tie the horns to the branches.

FOR THE HAT: Cut three holes in the top of a large plastic top hat. Cut three sheets of iridescent cellophane the same length as three decorated horns. Wrap the cellophane around the mouthpiece ends of the horns and gather it up into folds. Slip a horn into each of the hat holes. Working from the inside of the hat, draw the ends of the horns together and join them with a rubber band, angling the horns outward. Perch the hat on the top tree branch

113

bit-of-bubbly party favors

Turn little bottles into glittery snow globes, *left*. The secret is to thicken the water with corn syrup so the glitter and confetti move slowly through the colored liquid.

Mix two parts of light corn syrup with one part of distilled water. Add food coloring to the liquid. Purchase 2-ounce bottles that resemble champagne bottles in shape. Empty out and wash the bottles and remove the labels. Fill each bottle half full. Add glitter and confetti, then fill the bottle to the top with distilled water. Glue the cap to the bottle with industrial-strength glue. Shake the bottle to completely mix the liquids. Wrap a gold cupcake liner around the top of the bottle and glue it in place.

Print a label for each bottle and cut it out. Attach the label to the bottle with glue or double-sided tape. If desired, place each bottle in a silver votive cup that resembles a champagne bucket.

114

secret-fortune napkin ring

Write a special wish or New Year's prediction for each guest, tuck it into an envelope, and tie it to the napkin for a combination place card and napkin ring, *top right* . For fun, add a miniature champagne bottle.

Write your message on a colorful miniature gift card, then place the card in its envelope. Write the guest's name on the envelope. Punch a hole in the upper right corner of the envelope and card. Weave silver wire-edged ribbon through the hole and around the napkin. Tie the ribbon ends into a bow, catching the neck of the miniature champagne bottle in the knot of the bow.

salute!

Miniature top hats and tiny champagne bottles from the wedding and novelty aisles, *bottom right,* dress the tree for the night's party. Tie shiny metallic wired ribbon around each hat to form a band, shaping it into a bow at the back. Hold the ribbon in place with a dot of hot glue. Using a paper punch, make a hole in the front and back of each hat brim. Slip fine-gauge wire through the holes and attach the hat to the tree. Tie miniature champagne bottles to the tree with silver cord or ribbon.

mirror, mirror

Candlelight sparkles more magically than ever when surrounded by mirrors. Ornaments made from mirrors or prisms dangle from clear glass cylinder vases or hurricanes to reflect the flames of the candles and lights of the room. A large pillar candle provides the twinkle in the largest cylinder, while disco-ball-style ornaments offer lots of sparkle in the remainder of the vases. Place each vase on a mirrored candle plate, then add more plates around the table. Top some with votive cups and tea lights and others with ornaments that match those on the tree.

To make the mirrored strands, purchase inexpensive ornaments made up of tiny mirrored pieces or prisms. Cut the ornaments apart to make smaller strands. See the photographs *above* and on *page 19*. Add a spiral-style paper clip to the top of the ornament strand, then clip the strand over the edge of the cylinder. *Note:* If mirrored ornaments are not available, cut pieces of mirror (available at crafts stores) into small shapes using a glass-cutting tool. Glue the pieces back-to-back with monofilament sandwiched between the pieces, creating strands of mirrored shapes. Add prisms or clear beads as desired.

HAVE A BALL Gold and silver ornaments packed into a tight strand add sparkle to a small side window. Either glass or plastic ornaments will work, but the plastic ornaments will be less likely to break when you're handling the garland or if the balls come loose from the strand. Install a curtain tieback at each upper corner of the window. Place the tiebacks just outside the window frame with the ends facing upward. See the photograph at *left* for details. Cut a length of chain long enough to swag between the tiebacks and hang down on each side. If desired, hot-glue the cap of each ornament to the ornament. Attach each ornament to the chain with narrow silver-colored wire. Group the balls by color or mix them randomly. After the chain is full, mist the garland with matte finish spray to give some balls a frosted look. Carefully hang the garland from the tiebacks.

IN A TWINKLING
around the house

DOWN TO THE WIRE Bring wire garden edging out from winter storage and give it a new purpose for the holidays. The upper loops are perfect for holding cards and photos. Cut two matching strips of narrow corrugated cardboard the same length as the lower edge of the fencing. Sandwich the edging legs between the cardboard strips and glue the strips together.

GET LOOPY A trio of garlands with snowy designs gives a wintry look to a window, *far right*. Loop one garland along a drapery rod so each loop hangs at approximately the same length and the loops are evenly spaced. Secure the upper edges to the rod with thin wire. Repeat with the second and third strands. Cover the wires with sheer ribbon ties.

LIGHT DRESSING Swaddled in sheer fabric, white tree lights give off a soft glow, *above*. Loosely wrap white fabric, such as cheesecloth, tulle, or drapery sheer, around white-corded clear miniature lights. Install small hooks, nails, or drapery brackets at both upper corners of the window frame. Swag the light-filled fabric between the corners. Add satin bows and silver foliage to each corner. Be sure to use cool-burning lights.

SHEER MAGIC A sheer tablecloth with star cutouts lets the cloth underneath shine through, giving a small table an elegant look, *above*. A wood-burning tool makes it easy, cutting and sealing the edges of the cloth so the openings do not fray. Purchase a 100-percent-polyester sheer curtain panel large enough to drape over the table. Draw the circumference of the tablecloth onto the curtain. Run the tip of the wood-burning tool along the line, cutting and sealing the edge. *Note:* Work on a heat-proof surface such as glass. Place the cloth over the table. Draw three stars in the center of the cloth. Cut out the stars with the wood-burning tool. To embellish the stars, run a fine bead of fabric glue along the cut edges. Lay narrow double-faced satin ribbon along the glued edges, folding the ribbon over on itself at the corners.

THE LIGHT FANTASTIC Take your holiday decorating all the way to the top by decking out the dining room or entryway chandelier. Securely wire one exquisite ornament to the center of the light, making sure it hangs low enough to be visible below the arms of the chandelier. Surround the rest of the chandelier with loopy bows of wide satin ribbon. If necessary, conceal the ornament wire with a narrower ribbon.

top-notch topiaries

Give credit to the British—they turned gardening into an art form with shrubs shaped into topiaries. Bring the same creative touch to your table with miniature topiaries made from the most unexpected items.

Most of the topiaries shown here start with a plastic-foam cone, florist's foam, and an empty base. Trim the florist's foam to fit the base and hot-glue it in place. Using tacky crafts glue or hot glue, cover the cone with moss. For cones elevated above the base, join the two pieces with a stick. Glue the stick into each piece. To connect the cone directly to the base, join the two with several florist's picks.

sweet nothings

What a treat. The topiaries *opposite* are made from frosting and candy. Pillar-style candleholders form the bases. For the gumdrop and peppermint versions, place a star tip on purchased tube-style icing. Run one or two rows of icing around the bottom of a 6-inch-tall plastic-foam cone and press the candies into place. Repeat the process, working toward the top. Place a single candy at the tip.

For the candy cane tree, run vertical rows of icing along a 6-inch-tall plastic-foam cone. Position the candy canes so they touch at the top and the curved ends are ¼ inch from the bottom of the cone. Fan the candy canes slightly so they're evenly spaced at the bottom. Attach three peppermints and a gumdrop to the top.

To attach the cone to the candleholder, spread a layer of frosting on the bottom of the cone. Press the cone to the candleholder, allowing the frosting to work as glue.

airy topiary

The wiry wonder at *left* is constructed from chicken wire. Cut the wire double the height of the container with a width equal to the circumference plus three inches. Spray-paint the wire gold. After the paint dries, shape the wire into a cone. Cut away the excess wire and join the ends with thin gold wire. Press the cone into the base. Insert pieces of seeded eucalyptus and white berries into the wire, leaving the topiary open and airy.

pining away

When turned on end, tall thin pinecones, such as the Sequoia variety shown *below,* form their own tree shapes. Spray a 10-inch pinecone with white paint. Mist the pinecone with spray adhesive and sprinkle it with iridescent clear glitter. Fill a mint julep cup with florist's foam as described on *page 118.* Hot-glue the pinecone to the florist's foam and cover any visible foam with sheet moss.

Glue small artificial apples, sprigs of yellow silk flowers, and pieces of eucalyptus to the pinecone.

by the bay

Fresh bay leaves curl as they dry, creating the fun flippy shape shown *above left.* Fill a 6-inch-diameter basket with florist's foam and cover a 12-inch-tall plastic-foam cone with moss as described on *page 118.* Paint a 16-inch-long ¼-inch-diameter dowel brown. Join the cone and basket as described on *page 118,* leaving 4 inches between the two sections. Glue sheet moss over the florist's foam. Insert twigs around the dowel and wrap them with wire to secure them. Working from the bottom to the top, glue or pin fresh bay leaves to the cone. Overlap each row to cover half of the row below. Add artificial red berries to the basket. Top the topiary with a purchased star pick. *Note:* It will take several days for the bay leaves to dry and curl.

tasteful display

Miniature pears, plums, kumquats, berries, and grape leaves provide a regal mix of colors *above right.* The arrangement should last for up to a week. If underripe fresh fruits are not available, substitute high-quality artificial fruit.

Trim off the tip of a 12-inch plastic-foam cone. To attach the fruits to the cone, cover toothpicks with wood glue. Insert half of each toothpick into the fruit and half into the cone. Starting at the bottom, cover the cone with rows of pears. Place a final pear at the flat spot on the top. Fill in any empty spaces with plums, kumquats, cranberries, blueberries, and grape leaves. *Note:* Use half toothpicks for the berries and hot-glue the leaves directly to the cone. Display the topiary on a footed cake plate or compote.

veggie delight

It's true, you can have your tree and eat it, too. The tall, slim broccoli topiary at left is a buffet centerpiece that doubles as a party snack.

Spray paint a 5½-inch-tall 4½-inch-diameter clay pot silver. Pack it with florist's foam as described on *page 118*. Cut the top 8 inches from a large narrow plastic-foam cone. Divide the broccoli into florets. Insert a toothpick into each floret and then into the cone until the cone is completely covered. Using half toothpicks, add cranberries.

Join the cone and bucket with a 13-inch-long ½-inch-diameter dowel as described on *page 118*. Cut a leek the same length as the dowel. Split the leek in half lengthwise and hollow out the center. Cover dowel with the leek, securing the leek with silver ribbon. Cover the florist's foam with moss.

swirls of pearls

Pearl garland gives an iridescent glow to the simple topiary at *right*. Spray-paint a 12-inch-long plastic-foam cone, artificial grape leaves, and a round container silver. Fill the pot with florist's foam as described on *page 118*. Bend the leaves over the rim of the pot. Top the pot with the cone as described on *page 118*. Cut silver-colored wire into 2-inch-long pieces and bend each piece into a hairpin shape. Starting at the bottom, wrap the bead garland around the cone. Secure it by sliding the bent wire between beads and into the cone. Completely cover the cone.

Spiral an additional bead strand around the cone, attaching it in the same manner. Hot-glue the top bead in place.

GIVING FROM THE HEART

Finding that perfect gift may be as simple as making a trip to the pantry or button box. As people attempt to simplify their lives and homes, useful gifts are often the most appreciated. Pretty embellished stationery, pushpins topped with buttons or charms, and home-cooked food gifts bring pleasure now and don't add clutter later. Package them with clever boxes, papers, and tags as pretty and personal as the gifts inside.

starry-eyed gifts

You can really be a star by giving these stellar gifts made right in your kitchen. Each heavenly gift is either shaped like a star or packaged with a celestial theme in a tribute to the sacred holiday star. Share them with loved ones this sparkly season.

124

Ginger Cookie Sandwiches

Trim lemon-filled cookie stars with white chocolate doodles and dots.

Prep: 1 hour   **Chill:** 3 hours
Bake: 5 minutes per batch
Cool: 1 minute

- ½   cup shortening
- ½   cup sugar
- 1   teaspoon baking powder
- ½   teaspoon baking soda
- ½   teaspoon salt
- ½   teaspoon ground ginger
- ½   teaspoon ground cinnamon
- ½   teaspoon ground cloves
- 1   egg
- ⅓   cup mild-flavored molasses
- 2   tablespoons strong coffee
- 2½ cups all-purpose flour
- 1   recipe Lemon Butter Frosting
- 4   ounces white chocolate or white chocolate baking squares (optional)
- 2   teaspoons shortening (optional)

In a large mixing bowl, beat the ½ cup shortening with an electric mixer on medium to high speed for 30 seconds. Add sugar, baking powder, baking soda, salt, ginger, cinnamon, and cloves; beat until combined, scraping side of bowl occasionally. Beat in egg, molasses, and coffee until combined. Beat in as much of the flour as you can with the mixer. Stir in remaining flour. Divide dough in half. Cover and chill in the refrigerator about 3 hours or until easy to handle.

Preheat oven to 375°F. Lightly grease cookie sheet; set aside. On a lightly floured surface, roll dough, half at a time, to ⅛-inch thickness. Using 1½-, 2½-, and/or 3-inch star cutters, cut into stars. On prepared cookie sheet, arrange cutouts about 1 inch apart.

Bake for 5 to 6 minutes or until edges are firm. Cool on cookie sheet on a wire rack for 1 minute. Remove from cookie sheet; cool on wire rack.

To assemble, spread flat sides of half of the cookies with Lemon Butter Frosting; top with remaining same-size cookies, flat sides down.

If desired, in a small heavy saucepan, melt white chocolate and the 2 teaspoons shortening over low heat, stirring constantly; cool slightly. Pour white chocolate into a sturdy plastic bag or a pastry bag fitted with a small round tip. If using a plastic bag, snip one corner of the bag. Pipe dots or drizzles on tops of cookies. Let stand until chocolate is firm. Makes about 24 (3-inch) sandwich cookies.

Lemon Butter Frosting: In a medium mixing bowl, beat 3 tablespoons softened butter with an electric mixer on medium speed until smooth. Gradually add 1 cup sifted powdered sugar; beat until fluffy. Slowly beat in ½ teaspoon finely shredded lemon peel and 1 tablespoon lemon juice. Gradually beat in 2 cups sifted powdered sugar. Beat in enough milk (1 to 2 tablespoons) to make a frosting of spreading consistency.

Ginger Cookie Sandwiches

Candy Cane Brownie Cupcakes

Top mini minty brownie cupcakes with dazzling chocolate stars.

Prep: 1 hour   **Bake:** 12 minutes
Cool: 10 minutes

¾   cup butter
6   ounces unsweetened chocolate, cut up
1⅓ cups all-purpose flour
1   teaspoon baking powder
¼   teaspoon baking soda
Nonstick cooking spray (optional)
2   cups sugar
4   eggs
1   teaspoon vanilla
½   teaspoon peppermint extract
1   recipe Chocolate Frosting
1   recipe Chocolate Stars or purchased milk chocolate stars

In a large heavy saucepan, melt butter and unsweetened chocolate over low heat, stirring constantly. Remove from heat; cool.

In a small mixing bowl, stir together flour, baking powder and baking soda; set aside. Lightly coat 1¾-inch muffin cups with cooking spray or line with paper bake cups; set aside.

Preheat oven to 350°F. Stir sugar into cooled chocolate mixture in saucepan. Add eggs, one at a time, beating with a wooden spoon after each addition just until combined. Stir in vanilla and peppermint extract.

Add flour mixture to chocolate mixture; stir just until combined. Spoon batter into prepared cups, using a slightly rounded teaspoon for the cups lined with paper bake cups or a level tablespoon for the cups sprayed with nonstick coating.

Bake for 12 to 15 minutes or until a toothpick inserted into the centers comes out clean. Cool in pan on a wire rack for 10 minutes. Remove from cups; cool completely on wire rack.

Spread or pipe Chocolate Frosting onto cupcake tops. Top with Chocolate Stars. Makes 8 to 9 dozen cupcakes.

Chocolate Frosting: In a medium mixing bowl, beat ½ cup softened butter until fluffy. Gradually add 2 cups sifted powdered sugar and ½ cup unsweetened cocoa powder, beating well. Slowly beat in ⅓ cup milk and 1 teaspoon vanilla. Slowly beat in additional 2 cups sifted powdered sugar. Beat in additional milk or powdered sugar, if necessary, to make a frosting of spreading consistency.

Chocolate Stars: In a small heavy saucepan, melt 6 ounces semisweet chocolate pieces and 4 teaspoons shortening. Cool slightly. Place the melted mixture in a sturdy plastic bag; snip one corner of the bag. Drizzle chocolate mixture onto waxed paper in small star shapes. Let stand until set.

Shimmering Star Shortbread

Showcase giant star cookies on a platter, tied with a ribbon.

Prep: 30 minutes   **Bake:** 15 minutes
Cool: 5 minutes

2½ cups all-purpose flour
⅓   cup sugar
1⅓ cups butter
¼   cup finely chopped pistachio nuts
1   tablespoon finely shredded orange peel
1   recipe Orange Glaze
Silver and/or gold edible luster dust or edible glitter (optional)

Preheat oven to 325°F. In a large mixing bowl, stir together flour and sugar. Using a pastry blender, cut in butter until mixture resembles fine crumbs and starts to cling.

Stir in pistachio nuts and orange peel. Knead mixture until it holds together and becomes smooth. (The dough will eventually come together while kneading from the warmth of your hands.) Divide dough in half.

Line 2 ungreased cookie sheets with parchment paper; pat each dough portion to ½-inch thickness (about a 9×6-inch rectangle). Using desired star pattern, cut out one large star shape and several smaller (2- to 2½-inch) stars from each half of dough. Remove dough trimmings. If desired, pat trimmings to ½-inch thickness; use 2- to 2½-inch star cutters to cut out additional small stars. Arrange the stars on parchment-lined cookie sheets.

Bake about 15 minutes or until edges are light brown. Cool on the cookie sheet about 5 minutes. Place waxed paper under wire racks. Use a large spatula to carefully transfer cookies from the parchment liner to wire rack to cool.

Spoon Orange Glaze onto cooled stars, allowing glaze to flow over the sides to cover. (Spoon up any glaze that drips onto the waxed paper and drizzle it onto the stars.) Let stand until glaze sets. If desired, brush with luster dust and sprinkle with glitter. Makes two 8-inch star cookies or about sixteen 2- to 2½-inch star cookies.

Orange Glaze: In a small mixing bowl, stir together 2 cups sifted powdered sugar and 2 tablespoons orange juice. Stir in additional orange juice, 1 teaspoon at a time, until of glazing consistency (2 to 3 teaspoons total). (You may need to double the glaze recipe to coat stars made from scraps.)

White Macadamia Toffee

Fill gift tins with colorful tissue paper to present this buttery toffee.

Prep: 20 minutes   **Cook:** 15 minutes
Stand: 3 minutes   **Chill:** 20 minutes

- 1 cup butter
- 1 cup sugar
- 3 tablespoons water
- 1 tablespoon light-colored corn syrup
- 1 teaspoon vanilla
- 1½ cups white baking pieces
- ½ cup chopped macadamia nuts, toasted

Line a 15×10×1-inch baking pan with foil, extending foil over edges of pan; set aside.

Butter the sides of a heavy 2-quart saucepan. Melt the 1 cup butter in saucepan. Add sugar, the water, and corn syrup. Cook and stir over medium-high heat until mixture boils.

Clip a candy thermometer to side of pan. Reduce heat to medium; continue boiling at a moderate, steady rate, stirring frequently, until thermometer registers 290°F, soft-crack stage (about 15 minutes). (Adjust heat as necessary to maintain a steady boil.) Watch carefully after 280°F to prevent scorching.

Remove pan from heat; remove thermometer. Stir in vanilla. Pour candy into the prepared pan, spreading quickly to about ¼-inch thickness. (Toffee will not cover surface of pan.)

Let candy stand for 2 to 3 minutes or just until set. Sprinkle with white baking pieces. Let stand for 1 to 2 minutes. When baking pieces are soft, spread over candy. Sprinkle with nuts, pressing lightly into melted white chocolate. Chill in the refrigerator about 20 minutes or until firm. Use foil to lift candy out of pan. Break candy into pieces about 2 inches in size.

Store candy in a tightly covered container in the refrigerator for up to 3 weeks. Makes about 1½ pounds.

Shimmering Star Shortbread

127

White Macadamia Toffee

Anise-Raisin Bread Spirals

Anise-Raisin Bread Spirals

Package flavorful spirals in a star-studded cellophane bag for gift giving.

Prep: 30 minutes   **Rise:** 2 hours
Bake: 15 minutes

- 3   to 3½ cups all-purpose flour
- 1   package active dry yeast
- ¾   cup milk
- ⅓   cup granulated sugar
- ⅓   cup butter
- ½   teaspoon salt
- 2   eggs
- ¾   cup golden raisins
- 1¼ teaspoons anise seeds, crushed
- 2   tablespoons butter, melted
- 1   teaspoon finely shredded orange peel
- 1   egg white, slightly beaten
- 1   tablespoon water
Granulated sugar or coarse sugar

In a large mixing bowl, stir together 1½ cups flour and yeast; set aside.

In a small saucepan, heat and stir milk, ⅓ cup sugar, ⅓ cup butter, and salt just until warm (120°F to 130°F).

Add milk mixture and eggs to flour mixture. Beat on low for 30 seconds. Beat on high 3 minutes, scraping bowl. Using a wooden spoon, stir in raisins, anise seeds, and as much of the remaining flour as you can.

Turn dough out onto a lightly floured surface. Knead in enough of the remaining flour to make a moderately soft dough that is smooth and elastic (3 to 5 minutes total).

Shape dough into ball. Place in a lightly greased large bowl, turning once to grease surface. Cover; let rise in a warm place until double in size (1¼ to 1½ hours).

Punch dough down. Turn dough out onto a lightly floured surface. Divide dough in half. Cover and let rest for 10 minutes.

Lightly grease 2 large baking sheets; set aside. In a small mixing bowl, combine 2 tablespoons melted butter and orange peel; set aside.

Roll each dough portion to a 12×10-inch rectangle. Brush with butter mixture. Cut each rectangle into twelve 1-inch-wide strips. Roll each strip into a spiral, buttered side in. Moisten and pinch ends to seal. On prepared baking sheets, arrange spirals 3 inches apart. Cover; let rise in a warm place until nearly double (about 45 minutes).

Preheat oven to 350°F. In a small bowl, beat egg white and water; brush onto spirals. Sprinkle with sugar. Bake about 15 minutes or until golden. Remove from baking sheets; cool on wire racks. Makes 24 spirals.

Cranberry Muesli

Friends will love this as a snack mix or with milk for breakfast.

Prep: 15 minutes   **Bake:** 45 minutes

- 4   cups cornflakes
- 2½   cups bran cereal flakes
- 2   cups toasted oatmeal cereal flakes
- 1   cup chopped pecans or walnuts
- ⅔   cup frozen apple juice concentrate, thawed
- 2   tablespoons packed brown sugar
- 1½   teaspoons ground cinnamon
- 1   cup dried cranberries and/or dried blueberries
- 1   cup chopped pitted dates

Preheat oven to 300°F. In a large roasting pan, combine cornflakes, bran cereal flakes, oatmeal cereal flakes, and nuts. In a small bowl, stir together apple juice concentrate, brown sugar, and cinnamon. Drizzle juice mixture evenly over cereal mixture, tossing gently to coat (the mixture will be wet).

Bake for 45 minutes, stirring every 15 minutes. Cool in pan on a wire rack. Stir in cranberries and dates. Transfer to airtight containers; store for up to 3 weeks. Makes about 12 cups.

Cocoa-Coco Muffin Mix

Ingredients layered in a jar turn into nutty chocolate muffins.

Prep: 20 minutes   **Bake:** 18 minutes
Cool: 5 minutes

- 6 cups all-purpose flour
- 2 cups sugar
- 1 cup nonfat dry milk powder
- 1 cup unsweetened cocoa powder
- 2 tablespoons baking powder
- ½ teaspoon salt
- 2 12-ounce packages semisweet chocolate pieces
- 2 cups flaked coconut
- 2 cups coarsely chopped walnuts or pecans

In a very large mixing bowl, stir together flour, sugar, dry milk powder, unsweetened cocoa powder, baking powder, and salt.

In 4 clean, dry 1-quart jars, layer ingredients in the following order: about 2⅓ cups flour mixture for each and ½ cup chocolate pieces, coconut, and nuts for each. Tap jar gently on the counter to settle contents. Cover and store at room temperature for up to 1 month. Makes 4 (1-quart) gifts.

Baking directions: Preheat oven to 400°F. Lightly grease twelve 2½-inch muffin cups; set aside. In a medium mixing bowl, stir together the contents of 1 jar; make a well in the center. In a small mixing bowl, beat 1 egg; stir in ¾ cup water and ¼ cup cooking oil. Add egg mixture all at once to flour mixture; stir just until moistened. Spoon batter into prepared cups, filling each three-fourths full. Bake about 18 minutes or until a wooden toothpick inserted in the centers comes out clean. Cool in muffin cups on a wire rack for 5 minutes. Remove from muffin cups. Serve warm or cool. Makes 12 muffins.

Marzipan Cakes

Use an hors d'oeuvre cutter to cut an orange peel star for a garnish.

Prep: 35 minutes   **Bake:** 20 minutes
Cool: 10 minutes

- ¾ cup all-purpose flour
- 1 teaspoon baking powder
- ¼ teaspoon salt
- ¾ cup butter, softened
- ⅓ of an 8-ounce can almond paste,* crumbled (⅓ cup packed)
- ¾ cup sugar
- 1½ teaspoons finely shredded lemon peel
- 1 teaspoon vanilla
- 3 eggs
- ½ cup sugar
- 2 tablespoons lemon juice

Preheat oven to 325°F. Lightly grease and flour six 4-inch fluted tube pans or individual tube pans; set aside. In a small mixing bowl, stir together flour, baking powder, and salt; set aside.

In a large mixing bowl, beat butter and almond paste with an electric mixer for 30 seconds. Slowly add ¾ cup sugar, beating on high about 10 minutes or until fluffy. Beat in peel and vanilla. Add eggs, 1 at a time, beating about 1 minute after each and scraping bowl often. Add flour mixture, beating until combined. Spoon ½ cup batter into each prepared pan, spreading evenly.

Bake for 20 to 25 minutes or until a wooden toothpick inserted near the centers comes out clean. Cool cakes in pans on a wire rack for 10 minutes.

Meanwhile, for lemon syrup, in a small saucepan, combine ½ cup sugar, ¼ cup water, and lemon juice. Bring to boiling; reduce heat. Simmer, uncovered, about 10 minutes or until a light syrupy consistency. Remove from heat.

Remove cakes from pans. Brush warm cakes with lemon syrup. Cool completely on a wire rack. Wrap individually; store in the refrigerator for up to 5 days. Makes 6 cakes.

*Note: For best results, use an almond paste made without syrup or liquid glucose.

129

Marzipan Cakes

Cherry-Chipotle Grilling Sauce

Cherry-Chipotle Grilling Sauce

Rustle up some campware and gussy it up with a garland of stars to present this bold home-canned sauce.

Prep: 45 minutes   **Cook:** 30 minutes
Process: 20 minutes

- ¾ cup chopped onion
- 2 cloves garlic, minced
- 1 tablespoon olive oil
- 3 16-ounce packages frozen unsweetened pitted tart red cherries, thawed, or 3 pounds fresh tart red cherries, pitted
- 1 canned chipotle pepper in 1 tablespoon adobo sauce*
- 2 cups packed brown sugar
- ¾ cup cherry juice blend
- ¼ cup rice vinegar
- 2 tablespoons brown mustard
- 1 tablespoon soy sauce
- ½ teaspoon ground cumin
- ¼ teaspoon salt

In a medium skillet, cook and stir onion and garlic in hot oil just until tender. Remove from heat.

In a food processor or blender, place one-third of the cherries. Cover and process or blend until chopped. Transfer chopped cherries to a 5- to 6-quart Dutch oven. Repeat with remaining cherries. Process onion mixture and chipotle pepper until finely chopped. Transfer to the Dutch oven.

Add brown sugar, juice, vinegar, mustard, soy sauce, cumin, and salt. Bring to boiling; reduce heat. Simmer, uncovered, about 30 minutes or until desired consistency, stirring often.

Immediately ladle sauce into 6 hot, clean half-pint canning jars, leaving ½-inch headspace. Wipe jar rims and adjust lids. Process filled jars in a boiling water canner for 20 minutes (start timing when water returns to boil). Remove jars from the canner; cool jars on wire racks. Makes 6 (½-pint) gifts.

*Note: Hot peppers, such as chipotles, contain volatile oils that can burn eyes, lips, and sensitive skin. Wear plastic gloves while working with peppers, and be sure to wash your hands thoroughly afterward.

Serving suggestions: Brush sauce onto poultry, pork, or lamb during the last 5 minutes of grilling. You can also serve the sauce as a condiment for grilled meats, such as burgers.

Gingered Cranberry-Pear Chutney

Suggest serving this sweet-sour chutney with grilled meats or poultry or ham.

Prep: 30 minutes   **Cook:** 35 minutes
Process: 10 minutes

- 1 12-ounce package fresh cranberries (3 cups)
- 1⅔ cups packed brown sugar
- 1 medium onion, chopped
- 1⅓ cups water
- ½ cup cider vinegar
- 1 tablespoon lemon juice
- 3 inches stick cinnamon
- 1 tablespoon grated fresh ginger
- 3 large pears, peeled, cored, and coarsely chopped (3 cups)

In a 4-quart Dutch oven, combine cranberries, sugar, and onion. Stir in water, vinegar, lemon juice, cinnamon, and ginger. Bring to boiling; reduce heat. Simmer, uncovered, 20 minutes.

Add pears. Simmer, uncovered, about 15 minutes or until thickened, stirring often. Discard stick cinnamon.

Immediately ladle into 5 hot, clean half-pint canning jars, leaving ½-inch headspace. Wipe jar rims and adjust lids. Process filled jars in a boiling water canner for 10 minutes (start timing when water returns to boil). Remove the jars from the canner; cool jars on wire racks. Makes 5 (½-pint) gifts.

Sesame-Citrus Vinaigrette

Choose star-painted glass bottles for sharing gifts of this zesty vinaigrette.

Start to finish: 40 minutes

- 2 tablespoons finely shredded orange peel
- 1 cup orange juice
- 2 tablespoons finely shredded lemon peel
- ¾ cup lemon juice
- ⅓ cup honey
- ⅓ cup cider vinegar
- ⅓ cup light soy sauce
- 2 tablespoons grated fresh ginger
- 6 cloves garlic, minced
- ¾ teaspoon salt
- ¾ teaspoon freshly ground black pepper
- 3 cups olive oil or salad oil
- 2 tablespoons toasted sesame oil
- ½ cup sesame seeds, toasted

In a large mixing bowl, stir together orange peel, orange juice, lemon peel, lemon juice, honey, cider vinegar, soy sauce, ginger, garlic, salt, and pepper. Using a wire whisk, slowly whisk in olive oil and sesame oil. Whisk in sesame seeds.

Pour vinaigrette into 6 clean 1-cup decorative glass bottles; seal each with a cork or a nonmetallic lid. Store in the refrigerator for up to 1 week. Makes 6 (1-cup) gifts.

Serving suggestions: If vinaigrette is made with olive oil, let stand at room temperature for 30 minutes before using. Shake before serving. Serve over green salads, vegetable salads, noodle salads, steamed or stir-fried vegetables, grilled or baked fish, and on sandwiches.

Cheesy Pastry Stars

Coconut Bonbons

What could be sweeter than a box of homemade candy? Pictured on page 65.

Prep: 50 minutes   **Cook:** 30 minutes
Cool: 1 hour   **Stand:** 30 minutes

- 1 cup sugar
- 1 cup water
- ⅔ cup light-colored corn syrup
- 4 teaspoons butter
- 2 teaspoons vanilla
- 1 14-ounce package flaked coconut (5⅓ cups)
- 14 ounces vanilla-flavored candy coating
- 2 tablespoons shortening
- 3 cups flaked coconut

Line a baking sheet with waxed paper; set aside. In a heavy 1½-quart saucepan, combine sugar, the water, corn syrup, and butter. Cook and stir over medium-high heat until mixture boils (about 5 minutes).

Clip a candy thermometer to side of pan. Reduce heat to medium; continue boiling at a moderate, steady rate, stirring often, until 234°F, soft-ball stage (about 25 minutes). (Adjust heat to keep a steady boil.) Remove from heat; remove thermometer. Stir in vanilla.

In a large mixing bowl, place the 5⅓ cups coconut. Pour syrup mixture over coconut; stir well. Cool for 1 hour, stirring occasionally.

For each bonbon, scoop a rounded teaspoon of coconut mixture and roll between palms of wet hands to form a ball. Arrange on the prepared baking sheet. Let stand about 30 minutes or until balls are completely cooled. If necessary to reshape, roll balls between palms of wet hands.

In a medium saucepan, heat and stir candy coating and shortening over low heat until melted. Using a fork, quickly dip balls, 1 at a time, into melted coating. Draw the fork across rim of saucepan to remove excess coating.

Roll balls in 3 cups flaked coconut. Place on clean waxed paper; let stand until firm. Refrigerate in an airtight container up to 1 week. Makes 42 candies.

132

Cheesy Pastry Stars

Tie a stack of savory stars with colorful ribbon for a thoughtful hostess gift.

Prep: 30 minutes
Bake: 8 minutes per batch

- 1⅓ cups all-purpose flour
- ¾ teaspoon dried Italian seasoning, crushed
- ¼ teaspoon garlic powder
- ½ cup butter
- ¾ cup finely shredded Asiago cheese
- 3 to 4 tablespoons water

Preheat oven to 400°F. In a medium mixing bowl, stir together flour, Italian seasoning, and garlic powder. Using a pastry blender, cut in butter until pieces are the size of small peas. Stir in cheese.

Sprinkle 1 tablespoon of the water over part of the flour mixture; gently toss with a fork. Push moistened mixture to side of the bowl. Repeat, using 1 tablespoon of the water at a time, until all of the dough is moistened. Form into a ball; divide in half.

On a lightly floured surface, roll half of the dough to about ⅛-inch thickness. Using a 2½-inch star cutter, cut into stars, dipping cutter into flour between cuts. On an ungreased cookie sheet, arrange stars 1 inch apart. Repeat with remaining dough.

Bake for 8 to 10 minutes or until golden. Remove from cookie sheet; cool on a wire rack. Store in an airtight container for up to 3 days or freeze for up to 3 months. Makes 32 pastry stars.

Serving suggestions: Serve pastry stars as a party nibble, as a dipper for creamy dips, or with soups or salads.

Apricot Syrup

Prep: 15 minutes **Cook:** 45 minutes

- 4 cups sugar
- 2⅔ cups water
- 1 12-ounce can apricot nectar
- 1 6-ounce package dried apricots
- 3 inches stick cinnamon
- 1 teaspoon whole cardamom seeds (without pods)

In a large saucepan, combine all ingredients. Cook and stir over medium heat until sugar is dissolved. Bring to boiling; reduce heat. Simmer, uncovered, about 45 minutes or until syrup consistency. Remove from heat.

Place a strainer over a large glass measuring cup. Pour syrup through strainer; cool. (Reserve apricots for an ice cream topping; discard spices.)

Pour syrup into 3 or 4 clean ½-pint glass jars. Cover; store in refrigerator up to 1 week. Serve over waffles or pancakes. Makes 3 or 4 (½-pint) gifts.

Corn Chowder

Prep: 10 minutes **Cook:** 10 minutes

- 1 4-ounce container dehydrated whole kernel corn
- ⅓ cup cooked bacon pieces
- ⅓ cup packaged instant mashed potato flakes
- 1 tablespoon instant chicken bouillon granules
- 2 tablespoons dried minced onion
- ½ teaspoon dried thyme, crushed

In a clean, dry 1-quart glass jar, layer ingredients in the order listed; seal. Store in a cool, dry place for up to 3 months. Makes 1 (1-quart) gift.

Preparation directions: In a saucepan, combine 3 cups water and contents of jar. Bring to boiling; reduce heat. Simmer, covered, for 10 minutes or until corn is tender. Stir in 2 cups half-and-half, light cream, or milk. Heat through; do not boil. Makes 4 main-dish servings.

Apricot Syrup

133

gifts from the heart

From the closest of friends and family to the neighbors, teachers, and all those who do special favors throughout the year, the gift list just seems to grow and grow. Check these pages for easy personalized presents.

We've gathered a collection of handcrafted gifts ranging from made-just-for-you treasures to those that can be produced en masse in an evening's time. New technology and improved products make crafting easier and more successful than ever.

mirror, mirror

Plain glass containers sprayed with mirror paint take on the look of collectible mercury glass, *opposite*. Spraying the glassware on the inside not only protects the paint from scratching but also gives it depth similar to the old-fashioned glassware. To create a pattern in the paint, apply stickers or painter's tape before painting. Make sure the mouth of the glassware is large enough to accommodate your hand and the spray-paint can.

here's how

Clean the glass thoroughly and wash your hands so they are free of oils and lotions. Mask off the top of the container with wide low-tack painter's tape to prevent the spray paint from drifting to the outside rim. For dots, apply round stickers (available from an office supply store) to the inside of the container. See the photograph at *top right* for details. *Note:* Permanent stickers work better than removable ones. For clear stripes, apply narrow low-tack painter's tape to the inside

Following the manufacturer's instructions exactly, spray the inside of the container with five or more light coats of Krylon Looking Glass spray paint, available in kits from crafts stores. Multiple light coats work better than fewer heavy ones and take less time to dry. After the paint is dry, apply three or more coats of sealer from the paint kit.

After the sealer dries, carefully remove the tape from the outside. See the photograph at *lower right*

for details. Leave the stickers in place. The backs of the stickers will create white patterns in the glassware. For clear stripes, carefully remove the tape from the inside. Although the paint bonds well and is sealed, take care when handling the glassware to prevent any scratching of the painted surface.

135

personal papers

Monogrammed note cards almost too pretty to use are tucked into a matching envelope for a truly personal gift. A pen covered with matching beads completes the package. Look for coordinating decorative papers at scrapbooking and paper supply stores; then combine them in different ways so that each card is unique.

here's how

1. FOR THE CARDS: Use purchased blank note cards or cut your own from card stock. Sharpen the crease with a stylus. Print the desired initial onto decorative papers and cut it to the desired shape. Cut decorative papers to fit the card and glue them in place. Add the monogram. If desired, add a layer of vellum to the card front. Further embellish each card with bands and borders of contrasting paper. See *photograph 1* for details.

2. FOR THE ENVELOPE: Cut lightweight poster board 1 inch wider than the card and long enough to wrap around the stack of cards, allowing for a flap. Clip off the upper corners to shape the flap. Fold the card into an envelope shape, creasing it with a stylus. See *photograph 2*. Cover both sides of the poster board with decorative papers. Run the stylus along the creases again to sharpen them.

Add bands of contrasting papers to the edges. Fold the envelope into the final shape and glue the sides in place. Cut strips of contrasting papers to cover the glued edges. Fold the strips in half lengthwise and glue them over the edges.

3. FOR THE PEN: Cut a sheet of supersticky tape to fit around the barrel of a plain pen. Press the tape tightly to the pen. Thread a beading needle with a double strand of beading thread, letting the looped end of the thread be the longest. Slip a seed bead onto the thread. Run the needle through the thread loop and slide the bead to the end to knot it in place. Fill the thread with 3 inches of beads, stringing them in a random pattern. Coil the beads around the pen and press them into the tape. See *photograph 3* for details. Continue stringing beads and pressing them to the pen until the barrel is covered. For the final 3 inches, run the thread around the last bead and back through several beads to knot it. Trim the thread. Using a circle of supersticky tape or a dot of glue, cover the end of the pen with a larger bead.

clips of the past

Personalize purchased or self-made linen hand towels by adding designs that reflect the recipient's taste and style. Clip-art images, available in books at stores that sell art supplies, crafts, paper goods, and books, cover almost any topic imaginable and are meant to be copied. A special transfer paper that works in computer printers and photocopy machines makes it easy to transfer the designs to any smooth fabric surface.

here's how

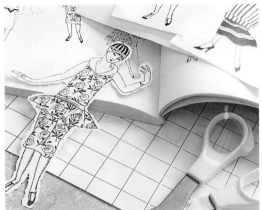

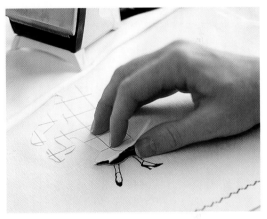

Enlarge the images to the desired size on a photocopier. The images shown are about 6 inches tall. Cut the images apart and recopy all of them onto a single sheet of paper. Following the instructions on the transfer paper, copy the images to the transfer paper. *Note:* Because brands and types of transfer paper work differently, follow the instructions exactly. Cut out each image with pinking shears or deckle-edge scissors, leaving a ⅛-inch margin of paper. See the photograph *above top* for details.

Following the manufacturer's instructions, transfer the image to the towel. For the best results, work on a hard, nonvented surface—such as a protected tabletop—instead of an ironing board. After the image is transferred, peel back a small section to see if the transfer is bonded. See the photograph *above bottom* for details. If it is not bonded, replace the paper and iron for an additional 10 seconds. When it has bonded, carefully peel away the backing. For transfer papers with silicone sheets, place the sheet over the image and iron again.

getting pushy

Perk up any bulletin board with decorative pushpins. Adding small items such as charms, buttons, or shells and placing the pins in a handcrafted matching box couldn't be easier or more charming.

Select 12 small coordinating toppers that are slightly larger than the head of an aluminum pushpin. If aluminum pushpins are not available, use clear plastic ones. For buttons, cut the shanks from the back using wire cutters or heavy-duty scissors. If needed, sand the back to make it perfectly smooth. Glue the embellishments to the tops of the pushpins using industrial-strength glue such as E6000. Let the glue dry overnight or longer

Paint or wrap a small box to match the pushpins. Add ribbons, strips of paper, or other decorations to the box tops. Cut a piece of plastic foam to fit snugly inside the box and glue it in place. Make sure it is shallow enough to accommodate the pushpins when the lid is in place. Cover the top of the plastic foam with matching decorative paper and glue it in place. Stick the pushpins into the plastic foam.

first-class delivery

Miniature masterpieces in the form of old postage stamps get a second life as wearable art. Copies of postage stamps (some including the cancellation marks) are available for purchase, or use stamps you've collected throughout the years. The stamps or similar images can be enlarged on a color photocopier for larger pins or reduced to make a cluster of small jewelry or earrings.

Apply clear self-adhesive laminate to the image; then cut out. Adhere the stamp to a scrap of ⅛-inch-thick foam core board with double-sided tape and cut away the excess board with a crafts knife. Follow the lines of the pin or cut the image into other shapes to make the most of the stamp's design. See the photograph *above* for ideas.

If desired, cut a scrap of 36-gauge copper tooling foil to fit the back of the foam-core board and join the two with double-sided tape. Wrap ⅜-inch-wide self-adhesive copper foil tape around the edges of the pin, mitering the corners. Press the foil to all the surfaces to seal it tightly; then trim away any excess. Using a stylus or a table fork, make lines across the foiling tape as shown *above*.

Add small beads, sequins, or other trims to beaded straight pins. Snip the pin shank beyond the beading to ½ inch. Dip the pin into industrial-strength glue; then press the pin shank through the foiling tape and into the foam-core board at the corners or wherever desired. Glue a pin clasp to the back.

charmed, i'm sure

Novel charms wrapped around stemware help guests keep track of their wineglasses and can serve as icebreakers as well. Word bubbles from the scrapbooking aisle spell out holiday greetings and add a bit of frivolity to the colorful dangles.

For each charm, cut a 10-inch piece of 18-gauge colored copper wire. Fold the wire in half and slide the cut ends into an electric drill as far as they will go. Chuck the drill to hold the wires tightly. Slip the loop end of the wire around an open hook, such as a cup hook. Slowly run the drill so the wire twists on itself. When the maximum tension is reached, the wire will snap clean from the drill. Remove the twisted wire

from the hook and the wire ends from the drill. If needed, lightly sand the ends of the twisted wire to remove any sharp edges.

Wrap the twisted wire around a ⅝-inch-diameter dowel or wooden spoon handle. Remove the wire and adjust the shape as needed.

Press a self-adhesive scrapbook word bubble to a bangle sequin. If necessary, add a small dot of clear industrial-strength glue such as E6000 under the bubble. Connect the bangle sequin to the loop on the wire with a 12mm jump ring.

To place the charm on a wineglass, slip the wire around the stem and twist it in place.

tiers of gold

Plain glass plates and inexpensive candlesticks make their way from the discount store shelves to the serving table when gold leaf and decorative marbles join them to make a triple-tiered server. Look for matching plain clear dishes in three different sizes to form the serving surfaces. Those with flat, narrow rims work best. Choose a pair of short glass candlesticks to separate the plates, making sure both the top and bottom edges of the candlesticks are flat and smooth.

here's how

Thoroughly wash and dry the plates. Paint the underside of each with gold leaf adhesive and let it dry until clear and tacky, following the manufacturer's directions. Cut waxed paper slightly larger than the squares of composition gold leaf. Place the waxed paper over a single sheet of gold leaf; then carefully lift it away. The static from the waxed paper will hold the leaf in place. See *photograph 1* for details.

Lay the leaf over the plate and press it into the adhesive. *Note:* Elevating the plate on a mug will make it easier to work around the edges. Using the waxed paper and light pressure, seal the leaf to the plate. See *photograph 2* for details.

Peel off the waxed paper. See *photograph 3* for details. Add more sheets of leaf until the plate is covered. The sheets can overlap (they will not seal together), and joints may be slightly visible. Fill in any small gaps with scraps of leaf. Using a soft brush, remove any excess leaf. Seal the leaf with several coats of spray gold leaf sealer.

After the sealer dries, turn the plate over and use glass-and-bead glue to attach flat-sided clear decorative marbles to the rim of each plate. See the photograph *above* for details. Work in small sections so the marbles do not slip while the glue dries.

When the marbles are tightly sealed, use industrial-strength glue such as E6000 or commercial glass-to-glass glue (available at glass stores and workshops) to glue the candlesticks between the plates. Make sure the candlesticks are centered; do not move them once they are in place. Let the glue dry for several days.

Take care when handling the server and wiping the gold surface. If desired, glue small felt pads to the underside of the bottom plate to prevent the leaf from being scratched if the plate is moved.

gift wraps

Who says presents have to come in cardboard boxes? Look to pretty containers when wrapping your gifts this year, then add colorful ribbons and tiny trims for extra personality.

Turn a trip to the flea market into a gift wrapping spree. Boxes, bottles, tins, and bags can become part of the present when used in creative ways. Interesting containers are often tucked away in workshops, garages, and attics, too. Don't hide the creative containers when you do your wrapping. Embellish them with ribbons, greens, ornaments, or flowers to enhance the unusual packaging.

box it up

Protect those fragile holiday gifts with wooden boxes. New boxes from the crafts store need decorating, but vintage ones already sport distinct personalities. A cigar box is tied with ribbon so a bit of the label shows. Pinecones are added to echo the natural tones of the box. A small woodburned crate is wound with ribbon and embellished with a bit of greenery, *opposite*.

do the cancan

You can find empty, unlabeled paint cans (for mixing up glazes and custom colors) at paint departments and paint stores. This year, stir a little fun into your holiday by packing gifts in the shiny containers as shown at *left*. Add bows, ornaments, or other trims to gussy up the hardware. The sturdy cans work especially well for protecting fragile gifts that have to be shipped. Don't forget to include the opener. Tie it to the handle with a ribbon or cord so it doesn't get misplaced in the gift-opening frenzy.

143

tin treasures

Old tin canisters often were as pretty as the merchandise inside. Employ these hardworking pieces as package wraps by adding some ribbon, trims, and a bit of greenery, *right*. After the holidays, they can go on display or back to work as planters, vases, or storage containers.

for deer ones

A simple celluloid reindeer hanging from looped ribbon dresses up a green glass jar, *opposite*. Both the jar and ornament can be found at flea markets and antiques malls for the cost of a box, paper, and bow. Fill the jar with edible goodies or tuck in a bit of tissue paper and slip a small gift inside.

in the bag

A gift certificate, crisp currency, or tickets for an evening out deserve more than a plain envelope or stock card. Tuck them into an evening bag salvaged from the back of the closet or a secondhand store. Wrap the bag with velvet or satin ribbon and add some sprigs of holly *left,* and the presentation is as heart-warming as the gift inside,.

SNOW MUCH FUN Take the easy way out and purchase this felt snowman *left* from the scrapbooking aisle to embellish a gift tag. If you prefer, make your own snowman from felt scraps, twigs, and pearl cotton. Glue your snowman to felt-covered card stock. Add long stitches for both function and fancy. Punch a hole in one corner of the tag and add an eyelet for strength.

GETTING PUNCHY An oversize paper punch helps the snowman *below* take shape. Make one snowman from blue card stock and one from white. Cut the hat from the blue figure and use it to top the white one. Cut more blue card stock for the gift tag and layer it with torn silver metallic paper. Glue the snowman to the silver paper. Add eyelets for buttons and embroidery stitches done with pearl cotton for the arms and face.

IN A TWINKLING
gift tags

DE-LIGHT-FUL A tiny tree topped with rhinestones adds sparkle to any package. Purchase a ready-made tree shape or make the tree from card stock using a paper punch, template, or your own design. Glue the tree to more card stock. For interest, add some torn paper between this layer and the final tag. Glue small flat-backed rhinestones to the tree.

GIVE IT A RAISE Lift up your design with embossing gel and powder, *above left*. Trace a hangtag onto card stock and cut it out. Stamp the reindeer face with embossing gel, apply silver embossing powder, and heat according to the manufacturer's directions. Repeat the process, applying embossing gel and red embossing powder to the nose. Add a cord with small jingle bells tied to the ends.

PLAY TAG A ring tag from the office supply store takes on a whole new personality when topped with card stock and a tree-shaped button, *above right*. Glue all the elements in place, then add a star-shaped eyelet for hanging.

147

CHARMED, I'M SURE A scrapbooking charm is all it takes to create the candy cane tag *above*. Hang the charm from a ring and tie it to layers of card stock using sheer ribbon. It couldn't be sweeter.

GETTING HANDY The mitten tag *left* warms your heart with its snowflake and tinsel trims. Cut a mitten from card stock. If desired, use a stylus to emboss around the edge and trace the raised portion with a silver pen. Add a tinsel cuff. Punch a snowflake from silver metallic paper and blue vellum. Attach the snowflakes to the mitten with an eyelet. Glue the mitten to card stock and back the tag with more layers of card stock. Join all the layers on one edge with three eyelets and lace them together with ribbon or cord.

KIDS' STUFF

Holidays and kids are a natural combination. Whether you're making projects for kids or with them, their creativity and sense of wonder make crafting more fun. Gather your supplies ahead of time and set up a work surface immune to paint spills, glue drips, and other messes. Be sure to offer plenty of encouragement and help explain the instructions, but don't worry if no one perfectly follows the examples shown. Making something imaginative and original is often a child's best contribution, so sit back and let the good times roll.

crafts for kids

Almost everyone is a kid at heart during the holiday season. Projects filled with wit and whimsy bring a smile to the face and a twinkle to the eye as soon as the crafting starts.

Whether the projects are done as a family activity, by the kids themselves, or as gifts for the little ones, having fun is what creativity is all about. Bright colors, jolly motifs, and simple lines make the season merry during both the making and the giving. Everyone will feel that joy when these gifts are opened on Christmas morn.

sock it to 'em

These snappy little fellows *opposite* sport true stocking caps made from the cuffs of socks. Look for bright-colored socks that have a bit of stretch. The faces are covered with socks, too, giving them a bit of texture.

here's how

Stretch a child's white sock (size 4–10 works best) over a 2½-inch plastic-foam ball. Push the ball into the toe of the sock and cut off the excess, leaving about 3 inches beyond the top of the ball. See the photograph *below left* for details. Using fabric glue, spot-glue the sock in place around the top of the ball.

Pull the cuff end of an adult-size sock over the ball to form the hat, covering the toe seam of the white sock. If desired, turn back the cuff to form a band on the hat. Spot-glue the hat in place. Cut off the remaining sock, leaving 4 to 5 inches beyond the ball for the stocking hat. Tie the top of the hat with yarn to form the proper shape. Glue or sew on small pom-poms, beads, buttons, jingle bells, or other trims if desired.

To create the nose, wrap orange plastic-coated wire around a sharp pencil. See the photograph *below right* for details. Make the nose as long or short as desired; bend it into a shape to fit the personality of your ornament. Glue the nose to the face. Glue black sew-on snaps or small black beads to the face for the eyes and mouth.

Lightly rub your finger in powdered blush makeup, then rub the blush onto the snowman face for rosy cheeks. Attach a thin gold wire for hanging.

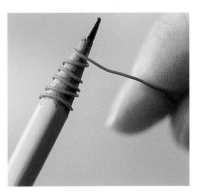

a banner celebration

Count down the days of Hanukkah with a felt banner. Each candle-shaped pocket holds a small gift for the nightly celebration. Our pockets are small, but make them any size you desire. Simply adjust the size of the backing and flames to fit the new pocket size. If pre-stiffened felt is not available in the size you want, substitute plain felt or other fabric, make a rod pocket in the top, and hang the banner from a dowel.

Round the corners of a 12½×18-inch piece of dark blue prestiffened felt. Use regular (not prestiffened) felt for the rest of the pieces. Cut turquoise felt into eight 2¼×3-inch pockets. Using stencils, computer-generated type, or your own design for the pattern, cut the numerals 1 through 8 and the word "Chanukah" or "Hanukkah" from raspberry felt. Cut eight 1¾-inch-tall flames from yellow felt.

Using fabric glue, adhere a numeral to each pocket. Arrange the pockets on the backing as shown in the photograph *below*. For interest, stagger the pockets slightly instead of using straight rows. Glue the pockets in place, leaving the tops open and allowing a little ease.

Glue a flame over each pocket, forming a candle. Center the wording across the top and glue it in place.

Punch a hole 1 inch from the top of the banner in each upper corner. Add a cord for hanging.

snow bowls

Use little dabs of ceramic paint to turn white soup or chili bowls into cheery servers, *opposite*. Both air-dry paints and ones that can be baked are available at the crafts stores, with some colors available in pen form to make painting extra easy. Give each little snow guy a different personality by changing the eyebrow or mouth shape. If you prefer soup or chili bowls to serving pieces, simply eliminate the earmuffs and scarves.

Wash and dry the bowls thoroughly. Using paints made specifically for glass and ceramics, paint black dots for the eyes, black X's for the mouth, and black squiggles for the eyebrows. Add an orange triangle for the nose, tipping or curving it slightly. Dip your finger into red paint, blot off the excess paint onto a paper towel, and rub cheeks onto the face. Cure the paint according to the manufacturer's directions.

Twist two chenille strips together for the handle. Using industrial-strength glue, such as E6000, glue the handle ends in place on either side of the bowl. See the photograph for details. After the glue dries, glue a matching 1-inch-diameter pom-pom over each chenille strip end.

Cut a 4×36-inch strip of wool for the scarf. Wrap the scarf around the bowl, tie it, and tack it to the bowl base with industrial-strength glue. Trim and fringe the ends as desired. Glue or sew buttons down the center of the scarf.

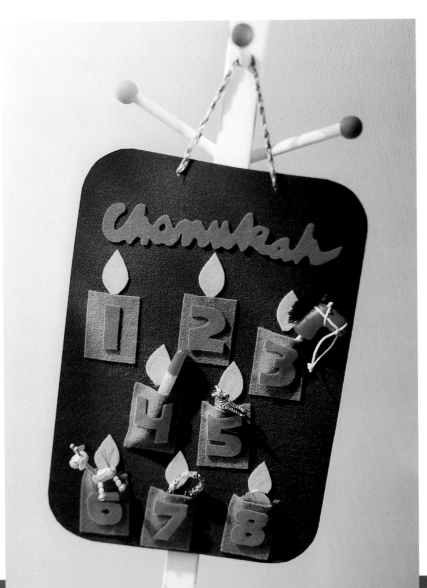

headed for fun

Warm up the young ones with fleecy headbands and scarves appliquéd with playful patterns, *opposite*. The mirthful moose and fluffy mittens are whip-stitched in place. Fleece fabric doesn't ravel, so there's no need to finish the edges. That makes both the stitching and appliquéing fast and easy.

MIGHTY MOOSE

MATERIALS AND SUPPLIES

Washable felt in the following colors: brown, antique-white, tan
8×60-inch piece each of red fleece and green fleece for the scarf
3×30-inch piece each of red fleece and green fleece for the headband
Fabric glue
Assorted red buttons
Two 5-centimeter round black beads
Fine-tipped black permanent marker
Black embroidery floss and a tapestry needle
Powder blush makeup

here's how

FOR THE SCARF: Enlarge the patterns on *page 157* to scale. Cut the head and two 1-inch squares from tan felt; the antlers and one 1-inch square from brown felt; and the forehead mark and two 1-inch squares from antique-white felt. In the following order, lay the antlers, head, and forehead mark in place on one end of the scarf. Glue them in place with fabric glue. Sew or glue the button in place for the nose and the beads above it for the eyes. Draw the eyebrows and mouth with permanent marker. Allow the glue and marker to dry.

Glue the five squares around the moose as shown. Glue or sew a button over each square.

Using three plies of floss, blanket-stitch or whipstitch around each piece. Apply powdered blush to the cheeks.

Place the green strip and red strip with right sides facing. Sew around all the edges using a ¼-inch seam allowance. Leave an opening for turning. Turn the scarf to the right side and slip-stitch the opening closed.

FOR THE HEADBAND: Measure around the child's head and cut the fleece strips to the proper length. The headband should fit snugly; allow for ¼-inch seam allowances. Cut two 1¼-inch squares from brown felt and two 1¼-inch squares from tan felt.

Center the squares along what will be the front of the headband, turning them on point to form diamonds. See the photograph for details. Glue the squares in place with fabric glue. Glue or sew a button to each square. After the glue dries, whipstitch or blanket-stitch around each square with three plies of floss.

Sew the short ends of each strip together, forming a circle. Place the red strip and the green strip with right sides facing. Sew around the long edges, leaving an opening for turning. Turn the headband right-side out and slip-stitch the opening closed.

MITTEN MUFFLER

MATERIALS AND SUPPLIES

Scraps of light purple fleece for the mitten appliqué
8×60-inch piece each of dark purple and light purple fleece for the scarf
5×30-inch piece each of dark purple and light purple fleece for the headband
Six 1-inch washable white pom-poms
12 inches of white satin cording
Fabric glue
Assorted white buttons

here's how

FOR THE SCARF: Cut two mittens from light purple fleece, reversing the direction of one so the thumbs face each other. Place the mittens approximately 10 inches from one end of the dark purple strip. Lay the cording in place to connect the mittens. Glue the mittens and cording in place. After the glue dries, use three plies of floss to cross-stitch or blanket-stitch around the edges of the mittens. Glue three pom-poms to the cuff of each mitten. Sew or glue buttons along the end of the scarf, keeping the last 8 inches of scarf free of buttons.

Lay one of the scarf pieces atop the other, right sides facing. Cut each end into eight 1-inch-wide strips, each about 6 inches long. This will form the fringe. Sew the scarf pieces together along the long edges, using a ¼-inch seam allowance and keeping the fringed portions free. Turn the scarf to the right side. Tie the upper and lower strips together in pairs to form knotted fringe.

FOR THE HEADBAND: Cut the headband pieces to fit as described for the moose head-band. Sew or glue buttons to the dark purple strip. Assemble the headband as described for the moose headband.

155

patterns

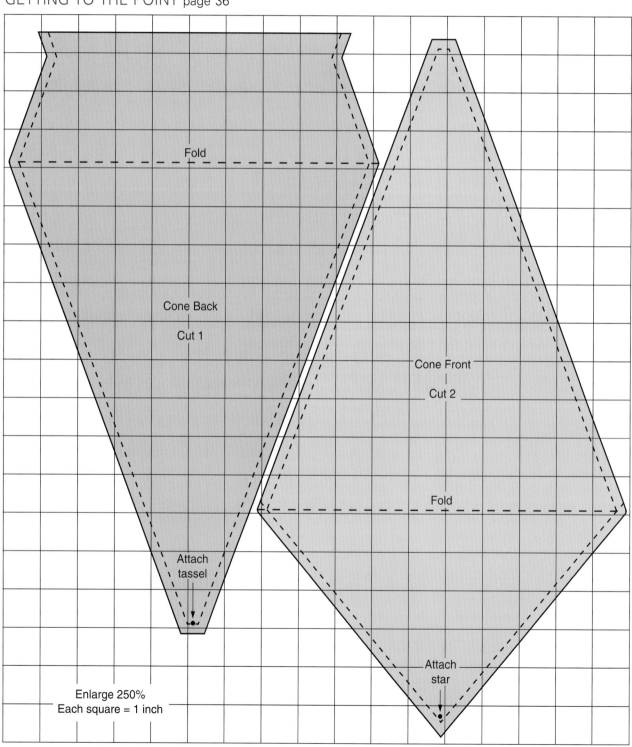

Fold

Cone Back

Cut 1

Cone Front

Cut 2

Fold

Attach
tassel

Attach
star

Enlarge 250%
Each square = 1 inch

156

STATIONERY OBJECTS page 39

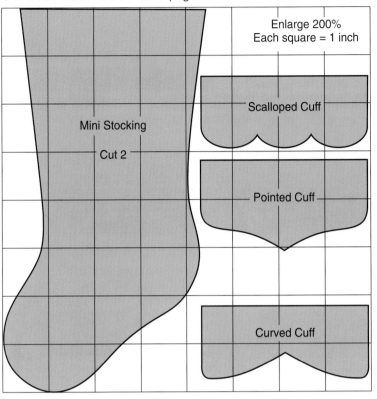

Enlarge 200%
Each square = 1 inch

Mini Stocking

Cut 2

Scalloped Cuff

Pointed Cuff

Curved Cuff

MIGHTY MOOSE page 155

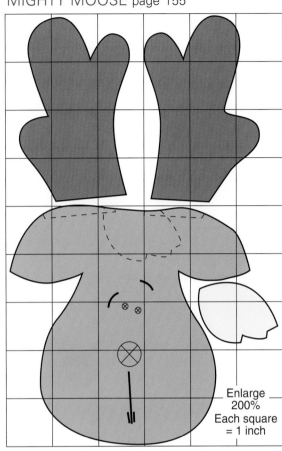

Enlarge
200%
Each square
= 1 inch

MITTEN MUFFLER page 155

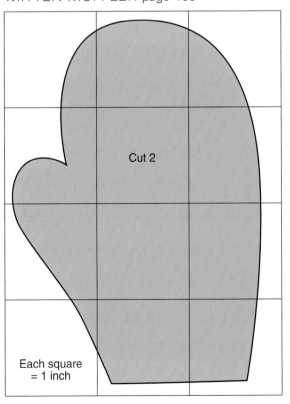

Cut 2

Each square
= 1 inch

DREIDEL page 66

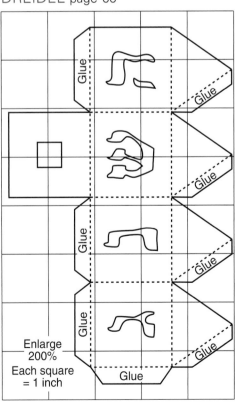

Glue

Glue

Glue

Glue

Glue

Glue

Glue

Glue

Glue

Enlarge
200%
Each square
= 1 inch

157

credits & sources

Styling by Marisa Dirks and Jilann Severson and photos by Peter Krumhardt except as listed.

Test Kitchen Photo Studio Director: Charles Worthington

cover: photo, Peter Krumhardt
page 4: photo, Judith Watts
page 7: design, Mary Jo Hiney Designs
pages 9–11: designs, Jim Williams; photos, Jon Jensen
pages 12–15: designs, Jim Williams; photos, Tria Giovan
page 16: top left: design, Carol Linnan; bottom right: design, Gayle Schadendorf
page 17: top left: design, Jim Williams; photo: Jon Jensen; bottom right: design: Joanne Lukens; photo, Jeff McNamara
pages 18–22: designs, Jim Williams
page 23: design, Jilann Severson
page 25: designs, Jim Williams
page 27: design, Betty Peachy; photo, Judith Watts
pages 28–29: designs, Jeni Hilpipre and Peggy Johnston; photos, Andy Lyons
pages 30–31: designs, Rebecca Jerdee; photos, Alise O'Brien
page 32: top left: design, Kristin Detrick; bottom left: design, Mary Jo Hiney Designs; bottom right: design, Heidi Palkovic; metal snowflake and tree embellishments (lower right): Boutique Trims, Inc., South Lyon, MI; poinsettia dimensional sticker (lower right): Jolee's Boutique Line from Stickopotamus, P.O. Box 1047, Clifton, NJ 07014

page 33: top left: design, Mary Jo Hiney Designs; bottom left: Julie Niederkorn; bottom right: design, Mary Jo Hiney Designs
page 35: designs, Mary Jo Hiney Designs; Chenille By the Inch by Fabric Cafe. 903/509-5999, www.fabriccafe.com
page 36: design, Kristin Detrick
page 37: design, Mary Jo Hiney Designs
page 38: design, Vicki Nail
page 39: design, Mary Jo Hiney Designs
pages 40–41: design, Jim Williams; photos, Jon Jensen
page 42: top: design, Jim Williams
page 43: designs, Vicki Nail
page 44: design, Jim Williams; photo, Jon Jensen
page 45: design, Jim Williams; photo, Bill Stites
pages 47–51: designs, Connells Maple Lee; photos, Perry Struse; stylist, Lorna Call; topiaries available for purchase from Connells Maple Lee, 614/237-8656 or 614/885-5350
page 51: bottom right: design, Camp Fire U.S.A. Clubs of West Des Moines, Iowa
pages 52–55: designs, Jim Williams; photos, Tria Giovan
pages 56–61: designs, Gayle Schadendorf; photos, Kim Cornelison
page 62: top left: design, Jim Williams; photo: Tria Giovan; bottom left: design, Gayle Schadendorf; right: design, Kristin Detrick
page 63: top left: design, Jim Williams; photo: Tria Giovan; bottom left: design, Jeni Hilpipre; photo: Hopkins Associates; right: design: Kristin Detrick and Heidi Palkovic

pages 64–65: food styling, Jill Lust
pages 66–69: designs, Rita Brownstein; photos, Tria Giovan
pages 70–77: recipes, Sandra Day; prop styling, Susan Mitchell; food styling, Dianna Nolin
pages 78–111: food styling, Jill Lust and Dianna Nolin
pages 112–115: designs, Vicki Nail
page 116: top: design: Gayle Schadendorf; bottom left: photo, Jon Jensen; bottom right: design, Gayle Schadendorf
page 117: top left: design, Gayle Schadendorf; top right: Jim Williams; photo: Tria Giovan; bottom right: design: Jim Williams; photo: Tria Giovan
pages 118–121: designs: Cody Bayard Evitt; photos, Hopkins Associates
pages 123: designs, Mary Jo Hiney Designs
pages 124–133: recipes, Shelli McConnell; photos, Andy Lyons; food styling, Dianna Nolin
pages 134–138: designs, Mary Jo Hiney Designs; papers (page 136): Anna Griffen, available at paper and scrapbooking stores nationwide; French Fashion Illustrations of the Twenties (page 137): Dover Publications. available at book stores and art supply stores nationwide
page 139: designs,Kristin Detrick
page 140: design, Jilann Severson
page 141: design, Jilann Severson
pages 142–145: designs, Jim Williams
pages 146–147: designs, Kathleen Paneitz; photos: Greg Scheidemann
pages 149–152: designs, Carol Linnan
page 153: design, Judi Kauffman
page 154: designs, Carol Linnan

index

index continued